To mon
Don + Carol

Memoirs of Pontius Pilate

A NOVEL

James R. Mills

Fleming H. Revell
A Division of Baker Book House Co
Grand Rapids, Michigan 49516

© 2000 by James R. Mills

Published by Fleming H. Revell
a division of Baker Book House Company
P.O. Box 6287, Grand Rapids, MI 49516-6287

Printed in the United States of America

Library of Congress Cataloging-in-Publication Data

Mills, James R., 1927–
    Memoirs of Pontius Pilate : a novel / James R. Mills.
        p.   cm.
     ISBN 0-8007-1773-2 (cloth)
     1. Pilate, Pontius, 1st cent.—Fiction. 2. Jesus Christ—Fiction. 3. Governors—Palestine—Fiction. 4. Jews—History—To 70 A.D.—Fiction. 5. Church history—Primitive and early church, ca. 30–600—Fiction. 6. Palestine—History—To 70 A.D.—Fiction. I. Title.
PS3563.I42315 M46 2000
813'.54—dc21
                                       99–051307

The map of Palestine on page 23 is from *Pictorial Profile of the Holy Land* by J. E. Holley and Carolyn F. Holley. Published by Fleming H. Revell Company.

For current information about all releases from Baker Book House, visit our web site:

              http://www.bakerbooks.com

Editor's Note

*P*ontius Pilate was appointed governor of Judea, Samaria, and Idumea in the year A.D. 27 by Lucius Aelius Sejanus, whom Tiberius Caesar had authorized to rule the Roman Empire on his behalf.

After Pilate had governed those provinces for ten years, he was arrested on a charge of murder by Lucius Vitellius, who was then the Roman president of Syria and, as such, was his superior. Vitellius sent him as a prisoner to Rome, to be tried before the emperor Caligula. That much is agreed on as historic fact.

According to an ancient tradition, the emperor found Pilate guilty and exiled him to Gaul, specifically to the city now known as Vienne. That tradition says he ended his life there by walking out into the Rhone River and drowning himself.

Contents

Prologue

*T*he time has come for me when I, like Julius Caesar, can say, "I have lived long enough, whether for fame or fortune." My wife is dead, and I have no friends here in my place of exile, so I spend my days reflecting upon the past, as old men do for lack of better ways to occupy their time.

As I reflect upon my experiences of long ago, I find that they are fading in my memory, losing their colors and details, growing as muzzy as wall paintings exposed to the elements in some ancient ruin. However, one action of mine is still as vivid in my mind as it ever was. I refer to my ordering of the crucifixion of that now famous Jewish carpenter called Jesus of Nazareth, while I was governor of Judea, Samaria, and Idumea.

Three years after I was exiled to Gaul by Caligula, that mad young emperor banished Herod Antipas to Lugdunum, just a few miles up the river that flows outside my window as I sit here writing this. Herod did not deserve to be disgraced, even as I did not, but we both had powerful enemies, and we both became the victims of those enemies.

Herod had been, like his father, Herod the Great, a loyal ally of Rome and a pragmatic ruler of his people. However, his youthful nephew Herod Agrippa was a close boyhood friend of Caligula's, and he wanted to be king of all the Jews, so the realm of Herod Antipas was added to his own, and Herod Antipas was banished to Gaul in his old age to die.

I had dinner with Herod Antipas once in the last year of his life, and we talked for over an hour about that strange carpenter. His wife was present, and she tried to turn our conversation to another odd Jewish mystic, one called John the Baptist, a fellow she had snared her husband into beheading. Herod muttered through his beard that it had been a mistake to kill John, which it clearly had been, and he spoke again of the carpenter, expressing a belief that the man's miracles had been genuine.

During the long years I have been in exile here, I have had few other occasions to talk about Jesus of Nazareth. However, an agent of the Emperor came here recently to question me about the man. The reason for that sudden imperial interest was, of course, the great fire that destroyed Rome.

I must acknowledge in passing that there are people who think the Christians are not guilty of the crime of starting that fire. Such skeptics say it is not in accordance with Christian principles to cause so much random death and destruction. Be that as it may, scandal mongers in Rome have been spreading a rumor that it was the Emperor himself who was responsible for the conflagration, and that created a need to assign blame elsewhere and to proceed at once with spectacular punishments.

Whether or not persons punished are responsible for the crimes of which they are accused is not the only factor to be taken into account sometimes. That can be an uncomfortable truth, as it was for me in the case of the carpenter.

It seems the Emperor wants to get rid of the Christians in any event. They have become subversive of the interests of the empire in their efforts to woo the general populace away from its beliefs in the officially recognized gods of Rome, including Nero himself, whose divinity seems important to him.

Punishing those wretches is easy to do, and watching them die provides popular entertainment for the citizens of the charred and blackened city. Because of the stories of their drinking blood as a part of their rituals, the Christians had already become objects of public loathing, and severe governmental condemnation became an appropriate way to appease that popular feeling of antipathy.

The current concern about this sect has caused me to sit down here at my desk with a long roll of papyrus, a lot of goose quills, and a pot of ink before me. My purpose is to spend a month of my otherwise idle time relating and explaining the events in the life of this fellow Jesus of Nazareth. I think it important to let readers know how the man was seen by his own people during his lifetime. Therefore I shall point out those peculiarities that set him apart from the other charlatans, demagogues, and zealots who have recently declared themselves to be the messiah, by which they mean the deliverer of the Jewish nation from Roman rule. Some of those pretenders have attracted considerable followings and have thereby caused a great deal of Jewish blood to flow. However, with the exception of this single individual, the execution of each of them has resulted in the disillusionment of his followers.

I'll give two examples. When Felix was governor of Judea, he had to deal with an Egyptian Jew who proclaimed he would bring down the walls of Jerusalem with a breath from his mouth. This shatterbrain presented himself east of the city, upon the Mount of Olives, where the messiah is expected to appear. He was able to assemble four thousand fools to attack the city, but Felix dispatched troops to take him prisoner. On the morning that maniac was executed, his movement vanished. Later, when Fadus was governor there, a magician named Theudas persuaded a multitude of Jews to go with him to the Jordan River, which he told them he would divide to allow them to walk through it dry-shod. To deal with them, Fadus sent a large detachment of cavalry which killed many of that mob and took a lot of prisoners. Among them was Theudas. The soldiers crucified him there on the bank of the river, and they cut off his head and took it to Fadus in Jerusalem.

Afterward none of his followers ever spoke of him again. It is surprising that a similar falling away has not taken place among the adherents of that carpenter, even though the measures now being taken to suppress them are thorough and systematic. The agent of the Emperor who came to see me here informed me that one of those who have been crucified in Rome recently was a Galilean fisherman named Peter who was a leader among them because he had been close to the carpenter. That imperial representative also told me that another man who had great authority responsible. The more his following grew, the more I had to take an interest in him, until at last he stood before me in the judgment hall of the Fortress Antonia on the last day of his life.

I remained as military governor of Judea, Samaria, and Idumea for four years after that. During that short time Christianity was already becoming a rapidly growing element among the Jews. Therefore I told my agents to continue to collect information about the crucified carpenter and the increasing legions of his worshipers. When I was dismissed by Vitellius and sent back to Rome to be tried before the emperor, I brought all that information with me, along with other material bearing upon the danger of messianic movements in that troubled land.

In addition, I still receive letters from the few friends I have left in Rome, and one of those friends recently sent me a biography of the carpenter that was taken from a group of his worshipers who were captured and then crucified in the arena in Rome. Fortunately that book contains a number of direct quotations of things the man said.

Because I possess these materials, and because I acquainted myself with the customs and beliefs and history of the Jews during the years when I was their governor, I can tell the story of Jesus of Nazareth and explain why he lived and died as he did.

Soon after my wife and I arrived
here in Gaul over a quarter of a century ago, she urged me to occupy my
time by composing a history of modern Palestine. She believed it might
be invaluable to those charged with
formulating imperial policies with
regard to the Jews.

Introduction

Soon after my wife and I arrived here in Gaul a quarter of a century ago, she urged me to occupy my time by composing a history of modern Palestine. She believed it might be invaluable to those charged with formulating imperial policies with regard to the Jews. Her suggestion appealed to me, in part because I wished to acquaint readers with how difficult it is to govern that tumultuous people, and in part because I wanted to justify the action for which I was dismissed as governor of Judea, Samaria, and Idumea, and exiled for life. After my wife died, however, I no longer cared what people thought of me, and I set that writing project aside.

It now occurs to me that some parts of that manuscript that deal with the strange religion and most recent history of the Jews would provide useful background information for understanding the life and death of Jesus of Nazareth.

Therefore I am offering here some of that work of long ago.

The Jews

No people are more widely scattered throughout the Roman Empire than the Jews. They are engaged in business activities in every seaport on the Mediterranean Sea and the Euxine. By choice they reside in their own quarters of each town, where they observe their curious customs and worship their strange god in their plain temples—or, to use their own term, *synagogues*. They have only one true temple. It is a gigantic monument in Jerusalem where hecatombs of animals are slain daily by their priests to propitiate their god.

The general antipathy that exists toward the Jews today arises from their self-righteousness. They offend every other people with their declarations that their god is the only real deity. Greeks, Egyptians, Babylonians, and most other peoples show tolerance with regard to each other's religions, if only out of common courtesy. We Romans go further, of course. We accept and worship any deity that appeals to us. We are willing to pay appropriate deference to the god of the Jews, but unlike other peoples, the Jews treat our gods with contempt, refusing to give them even the bare honors that respect for our feelings should demand. What is more, their vehemently expressed denials of the divinity of the emperors have caused them to be looked upon as subjects of questionable loyalty ever since Caesar Augustus was recognized as a god almost a century ago. The greatest concession they could then bring themselves to make was to offer daily sacrifices to their own god, asking him to look with favor upon Caesar, which must have amused Augustus, if he ever thought about it.

The Jews are incensed by the opinion of most educated Greeks and Romans that their faith is a bloodthirsty set of superstitions. They are also outraged by misconceptions about their religion that are common today throughout the empire.

We have all heard they believe in only one god, and that is correct. However, the widespread belief that the god they worship is Bacchus is not correct. That misapprehension has arisen out of a common misunderstanding as to the significance of a great golden grapevine that adorns the exterior of their temple in Jerusalem. There are also rituals they observe upon their feast days that are similar to certain rites of the bacchantes.

In a Roman bath, I once heard an intelligent man say that their unwillingness to eat the flesh of swine stems from their assigning divine attributes to boar hogs. That, too, is untrue. The reason they don't eat pork is because an ancient patriarch of theirs said that pigs are unclean, along with snails, oysters, lobsters, clams, eels, crabs, squids, and any number of other creatures for which the rest of us are thankful when they are properly prepared and set before us.

Apion the grammarian says the Jews offer to their god a Greek in sacrifice once a year in their temple and then eat his entrails after roasting them over a ceremonial fire. He also maintains that they worship an ass's head. I am surprised that Apion utters such nonsense. I dislike the Jews as much as he does, but I believe no good comes out of antipathies based on ignorance. It is better to hate people for what they are, rather than for what they are not.

The god of the Jews is a mysterious one. They believe him to be invisible and omnipotent. They think he is the creator of this world and the father of mankind. They believe he is present in the most holy part of their monumental temple in Jerusalem. That room is a windowless chamber behind a great curtain, a dark vault where no one but the high priest is allowed to go, and he can do it only on the most holy day of the year. Pompey entered that huge cubicle by right of conquest and found it to be quite empty. His intention was to seize their god and carry it back to Rome to hold it hostage there for the good conduct of the Jews, in accordance, of course, with the customary Roman practice after the conquest of a new territory. Naturally he was astonished to find there was no god to be seen and worshiped in that tremendous place.

One of the facts generally known about the Jews is that they believe their god has selected them to be his chosen people. That is a conviction that remains unshaken, even though their history is a long record of one catastrophe after another. This view of theirs is interpreted by other peoples to mean that the Jews are convinced they are better than the rest of us, but while they do feel superior, that feeling is no different from the good opinion every nation has of itself.

Jews are perverse about such things, however. For them, being the chosen people of their god is not so much an honor as it is a burden. In a characteristic passage upon the subject, an ancient prophet of theirs named Moses quotes their god as saying, "If you will obey my voice and keep my covenant, you shall be a treasure to me above all peoples. . . . And you shall be unto me a kingdom of priests and a holy nation." Elsewhere their god is represented as telling them, "I shall give thee for a light unto the gentiles." A central element of their faith is a belief in the eventual coming of a golden age when all mankind will live as brothers and sisters, as one harmonious family under the rule of their peculiar god. They believe they were selected to receive the laws of their god so they could set a necessary example for all the other nations of the world. They are convinced their god's chief concern is that they comply with the commandments they believe he gave them. They think an age of universal peace and brotherhood is deferred for the whole human race to the extent they fall short.

Another belief of the Jews relates to the land of Palestine. According to Moses, their god promised it to them as their homeland. It seems rather odd that they can convince themselves their god thinks so much of them. A god who cared for them should have promised them a land more fertile and richer in natural resources, rather than one in the path of every conquering army that rampages through that part of the world, leaving desolation behind it. Even so, Jews think it to be contrary to the will of their god that any gentile should possess one square foot of that arid land.

Their religion is based on five books attributed to Moses, as well as on the writings of other religious mystics from times long past. Most of those other authorities predict the eventual coming of a savior of the Jewish people. In their language he is called the *messiah*, a word meaning "the anointed one." In Greek the term *messiah* becomes *christ*. This leader is to come and deliver them from foreign oppressors and then reign in Jerusalem, not only over the Jews but over all the other countries of the world, in an empire that will be eternal—rather a heady concept for a minor nation that has been trodden underfoot for the last thousand years by one foreign conqueror after another.

Their messianic beliefs are yearning memories of a king named David, who was their greatest ruler. The death of his son Solomon marked the end of a mighty Jewish kingdom. Ever since then Jews have been dreaming of the return of the glories of that time. The messiah who is expected to fulfill that dream is to be a descendant of David, and Jews pray constantly for his early appearance.

Originally there were twelve tribes of Jews. After the death of Solomon, civil wars divided them into a southern kingdom of two tribes and a northern one of ten. After a few more centuries, the northern kingdom was conquered by the Assyrians.

Because the northern ten tribes became as trouble-some to the Assyrians as the other two are now becoming to Rome, King Sargon dispersed them throughout the Middle East. A few were allowed to remain within the territory of the northern kingdom, which included the land now called Samaria. Those who were left there soon began to intermarry with Assyrians and Chaldeans who had been resettled on the lands that had been depopulated, and because of their mixed ancestry, Samaritans have been despised by the Jews ever since that time.

A hundred years after the Assyrian conquest of that northern kingdom, the southern kingdom was overrun by Nebuchadnezzar II of Babylon, and the upper classes of the Jews were carried away into captivity in Mesopotamia, but after Babylon was conquered by the Persians, Cyrus the Great permitted the Jewish leaders to go back to Palestine, and many did so. Cyrus authorized the rebuilding of the city of Jerusalem, and he allocated funds to restore the great temple there. That generous action on the part of Cyrus caused an even more bitter hostility to arise between the Samaritans and the Jews.

It is the belief of the Jews that the mountaintop in the city of Jerusalem on which their temple is built is the place where one of their patriarchs, a legendary figure called Abraham, offered his son to their god as a sacrifice. When the Jews refused to accept assistance from the Samaritans in the rebuilding of the temple, the king of Samaria declared that Mount Gerizim in central Samaria was the hill where Abraham offered to slaughter his son, and the Samaritans undertook the construction of a temple of their own upon it. They performed their ritual sacrifices of animals there until the Jews conquered Samaria and tore down the building about a century ago.

During the six hundred years since Cyrus repatriated the Jews to Palestine, they have been the sullen subjects of the Persian, Egyptian, Seleucid, and Roman Empires, with very few interludes of independence. The last half dozen centuries have been an unending ordeal to them, because they have interpreted their repeated subjugations by foreign powers as evidence of their god's disapproval of them. That should have improved their behavior, but it hasn't.

The Recent History of the Jewish Nation

The social and political ferment now disrupting the peace of Palestine are the results of the military campaigns of Alexander the Great. His political heirs, the rulers of those empires that were created from his conquests, displayed the common inclination of sovereigns to appropriate assets that belong to somebody and present them to somebody else. The first Seleucid emperor granted entire Jewish cities to veterans of Alexander's victorious armies. That was done in part to reward soldiers for their service and in part to settle military colonies throughout Palestine in order to keep control of it.

The resentment of Jews who were evicted from their homes was intense, and they were even more appalled when cities from which they had been expelled were given new names, such as Scythopolis and Philadelphia, and soon became as Greek as Athens or Sparta.

The cynical sophistication of the invading Greeks was regarded by Jews as godless depravity. That and the renewed subjugation of their land by a foreign monarch made them rebellious.

Therefore the Seleucid emperor Antiochus Epiphanes IV decided to take what he considered appropriate actions to control the Jews. Knowing it was their religion that made them difficult to govern, he proposed to eradicate it. He prohibited various Jewish rites, including male circumcision, an odd practice of theirs. He also prohibited any observance of their holy day of rest, which occurs on every seventh day, and which they call the sabbath. He directed all commanders of his army of occupation to execute Jews who violated that decree.

He ordered that a colossal statue of the Olympian god Zeus be erected in the forecourt of their temple in Jerusalem, and—to add insult to injury—he posed for it himself. To completely profane that holy place, Antiochus directed that hogs be sacrificed on its altar. He also required Jewish priests to eat the flesh of those dead swine on penalty of death. Rather than commit such an awful impiety, the priests so ordered all chose to die, and they became the martyr heroes of the armed insurrection that flared up.

Under the leadership of a family of warrior priests called the Maccabees, the Jews carried on a bitter civil war against Antiochus Epiphanes. They managed to survive twenty years of atrocities and slaughter to gain their independence as a nation for the first time in four centuries.

The greatest hero among the Maccabees, a general called Judas, set up a theocratic government when he accepted the office of high priest on a hereditary basis. Before long one of his descendants assumed the title king of the Jews. The royal house he founded became known as the Hasmonean dynasty, and various classes of Jews in the new monarchy began to coalesce.

Surviving from the distant past was the priesthood, which had been made hereditary by King David. That religious hierarchy had become the aristocracy and the ruling class. Until recently only its members could sit as members of the Great Sanhedrin, which is the supreme tribunal of the Jews. Around that priestly caste grew up a political party called the Sadducees.

Originally they organized themselves as partisans of King John Hyrcanus to support his policy of foreign conquest, which was objectionable to many pious Jews because the materialism that was manifest in his imperialist policies did not seem to them consistent with what ought to be the aims of a nation ruled by a king who was also the high priest of their unearthly god.

The Sadducees soon filled all the high posts in the government of John Hyrcanus. They militantly supported his policy of reaching accommodations with great foreign powers, Egypt at first, and then the Roman republic. A conciliatory attitude toward Rome has been the touchstone of their statecraft ever since, and in recent years they have become increasingly unpopular because they still maintain that their nation must cooperate with Rome if it is to survive.

In addition to being the priests of the temple, they are the ecclesiastical judges, but they now find it politic to defer to the views of the Pharisees, who have become the prevailing party among the Jews. The Pharisees believe that quite a number of old books were inspired by their god, while the Sadducees think the only genuine scriptures are five books which are attributed to Moses. What is more, the Pharisees believe there is a life after death, but the Sadducees do not because Moses made no mention of it.

The Sadducees are the party of the priests, but the Pharisees are the party of the rabbis, who are scholars who study the Jewish scriptures in order to comprehend and interpret the laws of their peculiar god. The function of explaining religious laws has been relinquished by the priests, unwillingly, as the rabbis have come to overshadow them as an influence on religious Jews.

The name *Pharisee* was derived by them from the Jewish word for separated, because they separate themselves from those who are not also Pharisees. They are strict in their observance of Jewish law and are precise in its interpretation. Furthermore, they believe in a continuing development in the understanding of the law. New interpretations become binding for them by approval of an assembly of accredited rabbis. The result is that Jewish religious law has become more and more complex, and it is one of the eternal truths that any code of laws which can be amended by lawyers will in time become so complicated that no one but lawyers will understand it, and they will disagree.

In spite of their commanding influence upon Jewish religious thought, there are only about six thousand Pharisees. They follow no particular profession. They may be merchants, scribes, doctors, farmers, bakers, carpenters, fishermen, cobblers, or anything else.

Among the Jews there is also an odd monastic sect called the Essenes, who live in caves near the Dead support to Pompey the Great, who was then in the course of his triumphal campaign throughout the Middle East. Pompey sided with Hyrcanus but deprived him of the throne, leaving him only the office of high priest. The governing of Palestine was entrusted to Antipater, who had greatly impressed Pompey.

Antipater had shown good judgment when he allied himself with Rome, as then personified by Pompey. He did it again by deserting Pompey as soon as it was prudent to do so. As the fortunes of war turned against Pompey in his historic conflict with Julius Caesar, Antipater also turned against him. That judicious decision earned Antipater the appointment by Caesar as governor of Judea, and soon after he secured that position for himself, he obtained for Herod the post of governor of Galilee. At that time Herod was a youthful veteran of Julius Caesar's campaign in Egypt.

After the assassination of Caesar, Cassius gained control of the Middle East. Antipater and Herod promptly switched sides—and remained as governors of Judea and Galilee by serving Cassius. They did so by wringing more and more tax money out of the Jews to build up the military forces of Cassius and Brutus. In the course of that unpleasantness, Antipater was poisoned by an enemy. Herod then prevailed upon Cassius to put him into his father's place as the ruler of all the Jews.

After the defeat of Brutus and Cassius at Philippi, Herod went to Antony at once and appealed for forgiveness on the grounds that Cassius had given him no choice but to serve him. As the gods of fortune would have it, Herod and Antony had been great friends when they were both young soldiers serving Julius Caesar in Egypt. Antony was a practical man, and he welcomed Herod back as a friend and confirmed him in his father's position as ruler of the Jews.

Soon after that the Parthians invaded Judea and placed a son of Aristobolus on the throne there. Herod managed to escape with his life and nothing else. When he appeared in Rome as an exile, Mark Antony presented him to the senate and recounted his military services to Rome in times long past. Having already enlisted the support of Octavian, Antony moved that Herod be declared the king of the Jews. The motion carried, and Herod left the senate between Antony and Octavian on the way to a great banquet Antony hosted in his honor.

When Herod returned to Palestine, it was with the legions of Sosius, the president of Syria. After a long and bloody siege of Jerusalem, Sosius placed Herod upon the throne there.

During the early years of his reign, Herod encountered difficulties in hanging onto his crown. Once Cleopatra had seduced and bewitched Mark Antony,

As the king of the Jews, Herod had to put down one rebellion after another. He was abhorred by his subjects for being a ruler who had been imposed upon them by a Roman army. He was despised by them also because he was an Idumean. The Idumeans are an Arab people who, according to the Jewish scriptures, are the progeny of a man named Esau, the twin brother of a patriarch called Jacob, from whom the Jews believe they are descended. This Jacob is supposed to have cheated Esau and his descendants out of being their god's chosen people by misleading their blind father into thinking Jacob was his brother. According to the Jews, the result was that the blind old man gave Jacob a blessing he had planned to give Esau, and the children of Esau were thereby condemned to be the servants of the Jews—or, to put it poetically, as the Jews do, the hewers of wood and drawers of water for their Jewish overseers. The Idumeans are called *Edomites* by the Jews, who referred to Herod as the Edomite Servant because of his servile relationship to Caesar. Yet among Romans and Greeks he became known as Herod the Great as the consequence of his overcoming his enemies and extending the borders of his kingdom over all the land of Palestine. He further enhanced his reputation by rebuilding Palestinian cities and villages that had been destroyed by recent wars. Some of the finest towns in all of the Roman Empire today are new Greek cities he constructed. One splendid example is the present capital, Caesarea. In such cities of his realm, he erected temples to the Greek gods, an action that horrified the Jews. Herod also embellished his Gentile towns with other fine buildings as well as with forums, colonnades, and statues. However, he was not able to beautify any of his Jewish cities, since the law of Moses does not permit graven images or conspicuous decorations, and the Pharisees insist upon observance of that ancient code.

To try to mollify the hostility of his Jewish subjects, Herod embarked upon the most monumental of all of his projects, that of reconstructing on a grander scale their great temple in Jerusalem. As I have mentioned already, the result is magnificent. The Jews are immensely proud of it. A common saying among them now is that anyone who has not seen that structure has not seen anything really beautiful. Yet that splendid work did not diminish their hostility for Herod, because they detested the taxes he levied to pay for it and all of his other impressive projects.

Most of all, though, they hated him for having called on Rome to conquer them for him. The siege of Jerusalem that resulted cost thousands of Jewish lives. Everyone in that part of Palestine had had family members and friends among those casualties, and in their grief, all those Jews hated him with all their hearts.

King Herod offended his Jewish subjects in ways both major and minor. The Greeks were looked upon by the Jews as aliens who should not have any place in the holy land of the Jews, and they were still hated for having been oppressors of the Jews under the Seleucid emperors. Stories of the great atrocities committed by Greek soldiers during the Jewish wars of independence from Antiochus Epiphanes were told and retold wherever and whenever Jews met to talk with each other. Yet Herod surrounded himself with Greek intellectuals, because he preferred their company to that of Jewish intransigents. He even surrounded himself with Greek administrators to govern the daily lives of the Jews, and they hated that.

He sponsored Greek athletic activities and gave lavish grants to support the great games at Olympia. Finally, in recognition of his generosity, he was made the president of the Olympic games for life. Throughout his kingdom he built stadiums, gymnasiums, and hippodromes, even in the holy city of Jerusalem itself, much to the chagrin of the Pharisees. All religious Jews were appalled by the nudity of the participants in Greek athletic contests because there are strict prohibitions against nakedness in their scriptures.

So for all those reasons and many more, Herod was constantly reviled by his Jewish subjects. To keep them from further revolts, he built a number of fortresses at strategic points. In his early years as king, he erected an imposing one in Jerusalem, where its towers overlook the sacred precincts of the temple. He called that stronghold the Fortress Antonia, in honor of his friend and patron Mark Antony. The Fortress Antonia dominates the city and has come to represent the power of Rome, so its every stone is now a weight upon the hearts of the Jewish people.

All through the long reign of King Herod there was confusion around him because of the palace intrigues within his family. His wives and children and in-laws never stopped plotting against each other. He first married a Hasmonean princess named Miriamne, in an attempt to assure the undisputed succession of the crown to his descendants. Although she was young and beautiful, he killed her. He loved her more than any of his other wives, yet he ordered her execution on the basis of unsubstantiated accusations made by jealous relatives. At that same time he killed her mother and her grandfather, the former King Hyrcanus II. He also arranged for her brother to be held underwater when he went swimming in the palace pool in Jericho. The young man's offense was letting it be known that he intended to go to Egypt and seduce Mark Antony, who had an insatiable appetite for good-looking boys, as everyone knows. So Herod suspected the young man of planning to persuade Antony into making him the king of the Jews in place of Herod. Soon afterward Herod ordered the execution of Miriamne's two sons by him, bright young boys who were his favorite children and whom he had chosen to succeed him as the rulers of Palestine. He was killing off his children, his wives, and other relatives and friends until the day he died. Those incessant palace intrigues would have exhausted the patience of a philosopher, and King Herod, in spite of his passion for so many customs and sentiments that were Greek, never managed to develop a philosophical detachment about things that directly concerned him.

Out of his ever-increasing suspicions of almost everybody in his kingdom, Herod ultimately forbade his subjects to meet or walk or eat together in groups of three or more. He stationed spies in the cities and towns and out in the country to see if anybody met contrary to his edicts. Those accused of doing so were dragged away to one of the king's fortresses, and most of them were never seen again.

In his youth King Herod had been a handsome young prince, a fine athlete, and a daring warrior. The name his father had given him, *Herod,* is of course the Greek word for hero, and he was then altogether worthy of that name. As he grew older, he did what many handsome men do: he tried to conceal the external evidence of his deterioration. His clothes and his jewelry were more ostentatious than ever, and he kept his hair dyed as black as it had been in the days of his youth. Unfortunately Herod could not do anything about the deterioration inside his head.

By the time Jesus of Nazareth was born, King Herod was almost seventy years old, and he was slowly dying of a loathsome disease. He was bloated and full of pain and stinking with decay, and he was covered in various places with maggots, which were left undisturbed to eat his flesh where it was putrifying.

One of the last acts of King Herod was to issue an order that soldiers be sent out to arrest ten thousand prominent Jews from all parts of the country. Those distinguished men were to be captured and marched to the city of Jericho and impounded in the hippo-drome there. When those orders had been carried out, Herod directed that the ten thousand imprisoned men were to be executed on the day he died. He wanted to be sure there would be mourning among the Jews on that day rather than rejoicing, and that premeditated slaughter was how he proposed to achieve that end.

After he died, however, his order was not carried out, so no one at all mourned on the day of his death.

Editor's Note: Readers who wish to know more about the subjects covered in this introduction will find them described in greater detail in Volumes IV, V, VI, and VII of the First Series of The World History of the Jewish People, which were published in the 1970s by Rutgers University Press.

ONE

A Child Is Born

*T*hat strange carpenter came riding into Jerusalem on a donkey at the beginning of the last week of his life. He was greeted like an emperor by a madly rejoicing multitude, and the high priest of the Jews, whose name was Joseph ben Caiaphas, was alarmed. He was certain the fellow intended to raise a rebellion against Rome. I was not. Caiaphas therefore decided he should inform me as to why he thought Jesus of Nazareth such a serious threat to the peace of Judea.

He ordered a number of scholars to work all that night to produce a manuscript that described the circumstances and occurrences connected with the birth of Jesus, because those things were among the chief reasons for the concerns of Caiaphas and the other Jewish priests. He sent me that manuscript the next day. Later my wife became interested in the carpenter, so she insisted on saving that roll of papyrus. Therefore I still have it, and I present it here without any comments of my own.

To Pontius Pilate,
Procurator of the Provinces of Judea, Samaria, and
Idumea:
Peace be unto you.

During the reign of King Herod, the chief priests of Israel considered his reign a judgment of God that our people should bear patiently. Since his death we view the subjugation of our country by Rome in the same way. Some of the Pharisees agree, but most of them and their followers pray to God that He will soon reward their submission to His will by sending a messiah who will drive out our Roman rulers and restore the Jewish monarchy of David and Solomon.

According to most of the rabbis, the kingdom of God is now at hand. Among the books they accept as Scriptures is one which was written long ago by a man named Daniel. In it Daniel predicted the appearance of a messiah seventy weeks after Cyrus, the emperor of Persia, authorized the reconstruction of our temple in

Jerusalem. Rabbis have construed this prediction to mean weeks of years rather than weeks of days, and that waiting period of 490 years expired shortly before King Herod was placed upon his throne by the senate and the army of Rome. Consequently, some very dangerous ideas are gaining acceptance among the Jewish people. Political events and natural phenomena are being analyzed by rabbis as to whether or not they relate to the prophecy of Daniel. Most of those impractical scholars are agreed that the appearance of a messiah could occur at any time.

Specifically, the birth of a savior is expected. The author of another of those ancient books that the rabbis have chosen to accept as Scripture, a man named Isaiah, wrote, "Unto us a child is born, unto us a son is given, and the government shall be upon his shoulders, and his name shall be called wonderful, counselor, the mighty God, the everlasting father, the prince of peace." So it was into an ominous religious ferment that Jesus of Nazareth was born.

At that time a general census for tax purposes was under way in Judea. The man who is presumed to be the father of the child, a carpenter from Nazareth named Joseph, had come with his pregnant wife to Bethlehem, which was the city of King David. Followers of Jesus now say that Joseph was a descendant of David, and that is probably true. David had hundreds of wives, and he lived a thousand years ago, and Bethlehem is a little town, so everybody from that place is very likely descended from him, and Joseph was the lowly scion of a family from Bethlehem.

Since Roman law requires that owners of real property appear and pay taxes on it in the jurisdiction within which the property is located, Joseph had gone to Bethlehem because he had inherited an interest in a piece of land there. The location of the birth of the child is important because an ancient writer named Micah, who is another one of those men whom the rabbis consider prophets, predicted the messiah would be born in Bethlehem. If that fellow who rode into Jerusalem yesterday on a donkey had been born a week earlier—or a week later—in Nazareth, he probably would now be married and the father of a family and earning an honest living as a carpenter there.

As chance would have it, his birth took place at the time of an unusual phenomenon: the appearance of what seemed to be a bright star. Although it was viewed by ordinary people as remarkable, it was a natural occurrence, the conjoining of Jupiter and Saturn so that together they appeared to be one bright heavenly body in the constellation of Pisces.

After the child was born, three astrologers came to Jerusalem from the East, and those men were responsible for making a potent omen from what was a natural, though rare, occurrence. It is most likely that those men were Jews from Babylonia. They declared they had come to pay homage to the newly born king of the Jews. Who but Jews would undertake such an arduous journey across a desert to pay homage to a newborn Jewish prince? Their Babylonian origin is to be assumed because astrology is so popular among the Babylonians and because there has been a large Jewish population there ever since Nebuchadnezzar carried our ancestors off into captivity. A lot of exiled Jews had chosen to remain in Babylon when Cyrus the Great offered them the option of returning to the devastation that Nebuchadnezzar had so recently visited upon our land.

As the high priest of Israel, I put no faith in astrologers, but according to Jewish lore, Pisces is the sign of Israel as well as the sign of the messiah, and there is another sort of symbolism involved. Pisces is at the close of the old annual passage of the sun and at the beginning of the new one. Therefore all astrologers read into the appearance of that star the sign of the passing of an old era and the beginning of a new one.

Every one of the planets has a special significance to astrologers, of course. As for the two which came together in that conjunction, Jupiter represents good fortune and is considered a royal star, and Saturn is equated with our God by Jews who study the stars. Furthermore, the Babylonians teach that Saturn is the star of Judea and Syria. For all these reasons, the three astrologers took the temporary new star to be the sign of the birth of a Jewish king. According to contemporary accounts, the three men arrived in Jerusalem saying, "Where is he that is born the king of the Jews? We have seen his star and have come to worship him."

Their appearance and their questions disturbed Herod the Great. The kingdom had recently been agitated by a group of Pharisees who had gone about declaring that God had revealed to them His decision to drive the Romans out of the land of Israel and that a sign from heaven would soon signify the coming of a new king. Therefore, on hearing of the arrival of the astrologers in Jerusalem and of the question they were asking, King Herod called a number of priests, including me, to his palace. He was an awful sight, and he stank with decay. At once he asked us where the messianic king would be born. We felt threatened, so one of us responded by telling him Micah said the ruler of Israel would come out of Bethlehem. Herod then summoned the three travelers to appear before him, and he informed them that they should go to Bethlehem. He directed them to send word back to him when they found the newborn king, in order that he too might come and worship the baby. They responded to this expressed interest of the king with skepticism. When they learned the future king they had come to worship was not of Herod's lineage, they suspected the king would get rid of the child.

It was after nightfall when they left Jerusalem upon the road toward Bethlehem, and a second conjunction of Jupiter and Saturn, which occurred two months after the first, was in the dark sky over their destination. This new occurrence was taken by them to be yet another sign from God.

The astrologers found Joseph and his wife and the child in a stable, of all places. They presented gifts of gold,

frankincense, and myrrh. These costly items must have
been sent by rich Jews in Babylonia. Presumably a
collection had been taken up there after the meaning of
the star was construed as it was. The three Eastern sages
remained for some days worshiping the child. When they
left Bethlehem to return to their own country at last, they
did not go by way of Jerusalem, having correctly divined
the intent of King Herod in regard to the child.

When he received word of how that trio of starry-eyed
visitors had disregarded his order to return and report to
him in Jerusalem, the king was furious. He had never
hesitated to kill children of his own on the basis of
unproven suspicions, and he was even less reticent about
doing away with other people's offspring on similar
grounds. He therefore decreed that all male infants in
Bethlehem and its environs be put to the sword.

By this desperate decision the king compounded the
problem he was trying to solve. Because a slaughter of the
sons of Bethlehem is described in one of the books the
rabbis hold to be scriptural, that massacre has been
interpreted as an additional fulfillment of prophecy by
followers of Jesus of Nazareth.

Joseph was apparently informed by the three
astrologers of the king's interest in the child, so he bought
a donkey and fled with his wife and their baby down the
coast into Egypt. There are many villages of Jews in the
delta of the Nile. The refugee family may have stayed
among our countrymen in one of those small settlements,
or they may have gone on to the city of Alexandria, to the

Jewish quarter there. The expensive gifts the astrologers had brought to them would have given them the means to pay for lodging and food for a long time.

The deliverance of the child from death is now viewed by the man's followers as wonderful. It appears to them that King Herod had attempted to thwart the will of God by slaying the child and that God had intervened to save him.

The carpenter's supporters point out that another of our self-styled prophets, one whose name was Hosea, wrote, "I have called my son out of Egypt." So another alleged prophecy seems to have been fulfilled as a result of the murderous action of the king.

The common people of Israel have been taught by the Pharisees to believe in messengers of God that are known as angels. These beings are not mentioned by our prophet Moses in the holy books he wrote. If angels actually exist, we, the chief priests of Israel, are certain Moses would have mentioned them. He did not, so we do not believe in them. The carpenter's followers now tell each other of the appearance in the night sky over Bethlehem of angels that announced the birth of the future king of the Jews to shepherds in a field. Then the angels reportedly filled the heavens with hymns of praise to the newborn child. We assume this tale was invented later by someone who wanted to make the story of the birth of Jesus seem even more auspicious than it already appeared to be.

Be that as it may, those actual incidents which did surround his birth and that appear to be fulfillments of prophecies were undoubtedly pondered by Joseph and his

wife, whose name was Mary. In due time they decided to
tell their firstborn son about all of them. Perhaps they
thought he could be so inspired to become the means of
bringing to pass the dreams of their people. Of course,
that would depend on his developing the intelligence to
capitalize upon his portentous beginnings, and they
could hope for that.

The effects of their decisions upon their child were
profound. They both talked about contacts with angels
other than those in the sky over Bethlehem. They claimed
such messengers from our God had appeared to each of
them separately even before they left Nazareth to go to
Bethlehem. They said the angels had informed them
Mary's unborn child was going to be the messiah of the
Jews. They also declared that the angels had told them to
call the boy Jesus, which means "God saves." Joseph
claimed that the angel that had appeared to him in a
dream had told him not to hesitate to marry the woman
even though she was obviously pregnant. The angel
assured him, he said, that Mary was a virgin and that the
unborn infant was the only begotten son of our God.
Mary corroborated his story by reporting that an angel
had appeared to her at a well and had told her that her
baby would reign over Israel forever.

Skeptics made jokes about that tale of his being born
to a virgin, of course, but it is evident that Jesus himself
believed it and still does. No doubt he was teased as a child
by playmates about appearing in this world too soon after
the marriage of Joseph and Mary, and no doubt he took

pleasure from their explanation for the indecent earliness of his birth.

There are also peculiar tales told about the birth of another infant in Judea a few months before Jesus was born. This was the child who later became known as John the Baptist, the self-styled prophet whom Herod Antipas beheaded a few years ago. His mother, a previously barren woman named Elizabeth, happened to be a cousin to Mary. His father was an elderly temple priest called Zacharias.

This Zacharias announced that an angel appeared to him in the temple, while he was performing his priestly offices, to tell him his wife would conceive and bring forth a son who would become a great man of God. Those of us who do not believe in angels assume that vision of Zacharias was some kind of hallucination.

Word of an experience as remarkable as that of Zacharias would have been communicated to other members of his family and to those of Elizabeth, even to relatives as far away as Nazareth, and it is only reasonable to expect that those family members, including Joseph, would have given credence to the report.

The story which Joseph later told about seeing an angel in a dream could have been true. He may have had such a dream. In the course of our lives, we find a lot of our dreams relate to desires and fears that preoccupy us during our waking hours. It would not be surprising if that vision reported by Zacharias generated just such a dream during the undoubtedly troubled sleep of Joseph.

When a man is told by the love of his life that she has become pregnant without his involvement, it does not ordinarily make his sleep more tranquil, and the reasons his wife might have produced a concordant story, as she did, are obvious enough. The actual paternity of the child is, of course, open to speculation.

It is known that Mary spent some time in the home of Zacharias and Elizabeth while both of those women were pregnant. They surely talked about their unborn children then. Presumably they accepted each other's stories at face value. It would not have been courteous to do otherwise. One account of their visit includes a reference to Elizabeth's having accepted the child to be born to Mary as the messiah, in accord with Joseph and Mary's reports of their visions.

Further acts of Joseph and Mary added to the influences that would drive Jesus of Nazareth out of his mind and would move him to ride into Jerusalem on a donkey yesterday and would cause him to become a threat to our existence as a nation and as a people. After three years in Egypt the exiled couple heard of the death of King Herod. They returned with their child to the land of Israel but not to Judea, which had been bequeathed by King Herod to his son Archelaus. They were as terrified of him as they had been of Herod. So were we all.

Instead Mary and Joseph took the child to Galilee, which had been left by King Herod to his son Herod Antipas, who still rules there. They returned to the town of Nazareth. By so doing, they seemed to be fulfilling in the child a prophecy that the messiah would be called a Nazarene.

For obvious reasons it is important that you, as governor of this province, should know all these things about the birth of this fellow. I shall not exhaust your patience by telling you about his present doings. I am sure you are being kept informed about them, but I do want to inform you that the traditions about the messiah refer to his raising of the dead. The story that is now circulating about the carpenter resurrecting a man in Bethany is, therefore, a cause of great concern to me, and it should be to you.

In your next report to Caesar please inform him that the high priests of Israel pray daily for his continued good health

With all due respects,
Joseph ben Caiaphas

Editor's Note: The repeated conjunction of Jupiter and Saturn referred to by Caiaphas took place in the year 6 B.C., according to Johannes Kepler, and astronomers since Kepler have agreed to the correctness of his calculations. If that phenomenon was in fact the star of Bethlehem, the conclusions of early church authorities as to the year of Christ's birth were off by six years. That is reasonable to assume, since he was born during the reign of Herod the Great, and it is an established fact that Herod died in the year A.D. 4.

For the first few years I was in
Palestine, I was at odds with
Herod Antipas. However, we officially became friends upon the day
the carpenter was crucified, and I
soon found that I liked the old fox.
My wife didn't really, but she
thought he was an interesting example

TWO

The Boy Becomes a Carpenter

*F*or the first few years I was in Palestine, I was at odds with Herod Antipas. However, we officially became friends upon the day the carpenter was crucified, and I soon found that I liked the old fox. My wife didn't really, but she thought he was an interesting example of despotic knavery. Also, she had very little female company during those years, and his wife, Herodias, possessed a deadly sort of charm.

Whenever Herod and Herodias were in Jerusalem at the same time we were, they would invite us to take supper with them at the old Hasmonean palace, and we always accepted. They usually served us roast lamb, which we both liked, and the pleasure of conversation with them was considerable. The exchange of thoughts with social equals can be fully appreciated only by those who have been denied it for a few years.

Philosophically Herod and I were both Cynics. In the course of some of our evenings together, we talked about the teachings of Diogenes and Bion until our wives asked us to change the subject. Sometimes when that happened, I would ask Herod about some belief or custom of the Jews, and by that means I often gained from him useful knowledge about the practices and institutions of the people I was responsible for governing.

A month or two after the carpenter was crucified, I indirectly learned about his education in that way from Herod. As I have mentioned once already, I remember everything that has to do with that fellow clearly, so the following is an accurate account of that conversation.

As our dinner plates were cleared away that evening, my wife said, "We have had enough of Diogenes for one night."

I shrugged and said to Herod, "As I pass through towns in this country, I sometimes see groups of boys sitting on the ground in the shade of a tree. They are always paying attention to a rabbi, and I assume those sessions are their schools."

own interpretations of Jewish religious law into those boys' heads, and that is the reason the doctrines of the Pharisees have finally gained ascendance over those of the Sadducees." He yawned politely behind one hand and said, "You and most other Romans know that Jews won't work on one day out of every seven, but the observance of the sabbath day is not just a matter of taking a day off from work. Like other provisions of the Jewish law, this rule has been complicated by the Pharisees. Thirty-nine primary works of man have been enumerated and defined by them, and those are the actions that they prohibit upon the sabbath. Among labors specifically listed are all the ordinary ones men do to earn their living, like digging, plowing, harrowing, reaping, kneading, washing, sawing wood, driving nails, and tying knots.

"Stipulations relating to all those activities are detailed," Herod said. "For example, tying a knot will make a man guilty of breaking the sabbath, but there are exceptions to that rule. The knots of sailors and of camel drivers are forbidden, but it's not a sin if a man ties a knot that can be undone with one hand, and a woman may tie the strings of her cap, her girdle, or her shoes. So if a Jew wants to tie two things to each other on the sabbath, he can have his wife tie them to each other with her girdle without concern, but he would be committing a sin if he did it himself with a cord."

"That sounds silly," my wife said.

Herod again smiled faintly. "No food may be prepared on the sabbath," he went on, "and that involves having to know the rules as to which steps in the process of bringing food to the table are considered preparation and which are not. A rule that once made a simple distinction between cooking food and just warming it up again has been refined over and over throughout the years. It is now long and complicated, and it has become the subject of endless discussions and disputes that will undoubtedly continue until the end of time."

"I'm sure it will." Herodias nodded her head. "There isn't anything those Pharisees enjoy more than arguing with each other."

"The boys are also taught which sorts of vessels, utensils, tools, and furniture can be defiled and which cannot," Herod said. "They are taught that a flat plate with a rim can be defiled, but a flat plate without a rim cannot, and a round brass trumpet can be, although a straight one cannot. A wooden key with iron teeth is susceptible, but an iron key with wooden teeth is not."

"No," Herodias said. "It is the other way around."

"Perhaps it is," Herod responded, and he raised one hand and covered his mouth with it, and he again belched politely. "A stove will be defiled if wood from a grove sacred to one of the Roman or Greek gods is burned in it," he went on casually. "Any such old stove may be purified, but any such new stove must be broken."

"Do they learn anything useful in those schools?" I inquired of Herod.

The tetrarch smiled again, a little more broadly than before. "What do you mean by useful?" he said.

"Arithmetic, algebra, geometry," I replied.

"Those who get involved in some kind of business learn how to cipher," Herod responded, "but they do it at the place where they work. Not many of them learn anything about algebra and geometry, so the lovely logic of Pythagoras and Euclid has no influence upon their thinking."

"And none of them know anything about the arts," his wife said rather scornfully.

On an evening some time after the death of the carpenter, I asked Herod, "What do you know about that fellow's childhood?"

"Nothing in particular," he replied.

"Can you tell us anything in general?" I said.

"Jewish law makes it the duty of every boy's father to see to it that his son is capable of earning a living when he grows up," Herod responded. "Therefore it's safe to say Jesus learned the art of carpentry from

Joseph. He would have spent every afternoon in the workshop of his father, sweeping up sawdust and wood chips and shavings, and oiling tables and chairs and chests that Joseph had made for sale. When he was done with those chores and such other menial jobs, Joseph would have talked to him about whatever work he had in hand at the time. That is how Joseph would have taught him to use all of the tools in the shop, the planes, the chisels, the saws, the drills, and the draw knives. Instruction on the use of the adze would have come much later, of course."

"Why?" my wife inquired.

"Because it's easy to cut off your feet with an adze," Herod replied.

"Aside from his mornings in the village school, what religious instruction would he have had?" I asked.

"A lot," Herod said. "Joseph, like every other Jewish father, would have taken the boy to synagogue with him in the forenoon of each sabbath day. The services then consist of prayers, a reading of the Torah, and a reading from the prophets. All that would be in Hebrew. After each scripture reading, the congregation would hear a translation into Aramaic, for the benefit of those present whose Hebrew wasn't very good. That would be followed by commentary on the passage read. After a few hours of that they would go home for a midday meal of things that hadn't been fixed that day."

We went on to talk about other things—I don't remember what—but before I fell asleep that night, I reconsidered what Herod had said about the childhood of Jesus. As a boy sitting beside Joseph during those services, he must have listened with fascination to the scriptural promises of a Jewish king who would rule over all of the nations of the world in a golden age that would never end. At such times the boy must have been turning over in his mind the stories his parents had been telling him about the angels and about the star and about those predictions the three Eastern astrologers had made concerning him, as well as all those odd coincidences that made his birth seem to be a fulfillment of prophecy.

Jesus was educated by his elders to eat, sleep, and breathe their religion, and to be willing to live for it or to die for it. Such Jewish religious attitudes are hard for Romans to understand. A Roman will die for a cause or for honor or for Rome or just to show he is not afraid to, but I don't know any Roman who would die for his religion. Being practical people, Romans worship gods who do not demand unreasonable sacrifices.

Nazareth, the town where Jesus grew up, is three miles south of Sepphoris, the largest city in Galilee. Sepphoris was then also the seat of the government of Herod Antipas.

Nazareth is located in an amphitheater of arid hills just to the north of the Valley of Esdraelon. The narrow pavement of the Via Maris runs through that valley on its way from Egypt to Syria, Parthia, and Babylon. Caravans of camels can be seen carrying the wealth of nations over that straight highway.

On the afternoon of a sabbath, for relaxation, a family from Nazareth might walk into Sepphoris. According to some Christian accounts, Mary was born there, and her family probably still lived there during the years Jesus was growing up, so Joseph and Mary may have taken him there often to see his grandparents. On days other than the sabbath they would have visited the marketplaces of Sepphoris, where exotic foreigners were selling the products of faraway places. A longer walk downhill into the town of Nain in the Valley of Esdraelon would have taken them to where they could see the merchants and the camel drivers of many nations passing by on the Via Maris.

As an impressionable boy, Jesus would have learned that those travelers were devotees of mystery faiths of the East that involve resurrected saviors. In Nain he would have heard Egyptians singing in praise of Osiris, their lord of lords, whose return to life they celebrate joyously at the end of every winter. He would also have heard traveling Greeks rejoicing over Adonis rising from the grave in the spring of each year. The Syrian merchants who were passing through would have joined with Babylonians in raising their voices in exaltation of Tammuz, the divine husband of Ishtar, who died at her hands and rose to immortal life after three days and ascended into heaven. His worshipers greet each other and all the rest of mankind with the cry "The Lord is risen" at the beginning of every spring when they celebrate his resurrection. Osiris and Adonis and Tammuz are agricultural deities of course, like our own Persephone, who is also said to rise from the dead in the spring of each year. Agricultural deities all over the world allegedly arise to new life in springtime, but not in Jewish Palestine.

When the carpenter had grown up and had declared himself the messiah and had come from Galilee into Judea, I asked a few Jews what they thought of him, and every one of them told me they were disturbed by reports that he had said he would rise from the dead after three days. They all said that sounded like the religion of Tammuz, which had been denounced as an abomination in the eyes of their god by a writer named Ezekiel—who is another one of those ancients believed to be a prophet by the Pharisees.

Because it probably affected the development of some of the attitudes of Jesus, I should add a few words about the economic state of Galilee, and Palestine as a whole, during his childhood. Although the benefits of Roman rule have never been admitted by most Jews, they must all have been conscious of advantages of an orderly economy and a stable government under the principate of Caesar Augustus. The best roads the Near East had ever seen were being laid down, making overland commerce prosper. The seas had been made safe from pirates, so maritime trade was flourishing as never before. Everywhere the armies of Rome maintained order, so business thrived and farmers had markets for their crops. Moreover, the Jews of Nazareth were all aware their people were being treated better than the populations of other nations subject to Roman rule. This was initially the result of decrees of Julius Caesar, who granted them a number of concessions relating to their faith.

These concessions were renewed by Caesar Augustus and Marcus Agrippa. After voluntarily joining Agrippa with a mighty force in a military campaign on the northern shore of the Euxine, Herod prevailed upon him and Caesar to confirm the laws of the Jews. Their codes forbade them to appear in court upon the seventh day of the week. As Julius Caesar had done long before, Augustus and Agrippa excused them from all such appearances. The ritual observance of the sabbath, as well as compliance with their dietary laws, made it impossible for Jews to serve in Roman armies.

Therefore Jewish men were exempted from military conscription.

These singular concessions continue in effect until this day, and that is another reason for the unpopularity of Jews among most of the other subject peoples of the empire. And so it was that the carpenter's boy in Nazareth grew up full of awareness that Julius Caesar and Caesar Augustus, the two greatest men of the age, had acknowledged the special position of the Jews among the peoples of the world.

During this peaceful interlude in their troubled history, the fact that Jews were better off than they had ever been in the past did not diminish their hope for an early advent of their messiah. That hope burned as brightly as the kitchen fire in every Jewish home, especially in Joseph and Mary's abode in Nazareth, because of the star and the astrologers and the prophecies and all that.

As unpopular as Herod the Great had been, his death came as a blow to the people of Nazareth just as it did to Jews everywhere else, because all semblance of a national existence expired for the time being with him. The old king's last will divided his kingdom among three of the sons he had not yet murdered. Archelaus, who was almost as bloody minded as his father, was left Judea, Samaria, and Idumea. His authority over these lands was confirmed to him by a decree of Caesar Augustus with the title of ethnarch, which is a little less than monarch.

Hatred of Archelaus occasioned a revolt in Jerusalem when the carpenter was still a boy learning his trade from his father. He and everyone in Nazareth heard that rebels had seized the city and killed its Roman garrison. The legions of Varus, the president of Syria, soon marched down through Galilee on their way to Jerusalem. During his prolonged siege of the city, Varus crucified thousands of rebellious Jews on a forest of crosses just outside the walls to let the defenders of Jerusalem know what they could expect after the city fell, and the Jews of Nazareth heard about that too, of course.

After the death of King Herod, Nazareth became a part of the dominions of Herod Antipas, to whom his father had bequeathed all of Galilee and Perea. Herod Philip, another brother, got the rest of the Jewish lands east of the Jordan River. Both Herod Antipas and Herod Philip were given the title of tetrarch, which is a little less than ethnarch. One effect of the division of the kingdom by the will of Herod the Great was that the authority of the Great Sanhedrin in Jerusalem was limited to the territories of Archelaus, that is, to Judea, Samaria, and Idumea. Henceforth the inhabitants of Galilee and Perea, who were then ruled by Herod Antipas, were not subject to that religious tribunal as long as they stayed out of Judea, Samaria, and Idumea. That must be remembered if one is to understand the reasons behind certain of the travels of Jesus Christ during his life.

All vestiges of a Jewish national unity were wiped away when Archelaus was deposed by Caesar Augustus as a response to protests made by leading men of Judea against the ethnarch's insane tyranny. His realm was reconstituted by Caesar as a Roman province and was designated by Augustus to be an area in need of an active military defense because of its proximity to the Parthian Empire. Therefore the new Roman province was to be governed by an army officer nominated by Caesar, rather than by a civil governor appointed by the senate. The emperor named Coponius to be the first of the military governors, or procurators, to give the correct title.

Although they had asked Caesar specifically for that change and although they surely found direct Roman rule to be preferable to the mad tyranny of Archelaus, it was impossible for the Jews to accept rule by a Roman prefect on a permanent basis. That had not been what they had anticipated when they had asked Caesar to depose the ethnarch. As the permanence of Roman rule became more and more apparent with the passage of time, a restlessness began to develop in Judea, and during my ten years as procurator there, it broke out in the form of riotous disorders, some of which I shall describe before I am done with this account.

Galilee and Perea together were not large enough to be called a kingdom, but within them Herod Antipas possessed all the powers of a monarch, so his subjects customarily referred to him as King Herod. He had fortunately inherited more of his father's cunning and less of the old king's ferocity than Archelaus had. So he was careful not to invite hostility to himself as his brother had done. Yet the unrest in Galilee paralleled that in Judea. Herod Antipas, like his father, was a representative of Roman rule and was therefore perceived by his subjects as inimical to the autonomy of the Jewish nation.

The tetrarch in all of his splendor was undoubtedly seen from time to time by Jesus, growing up as he did just three miles from Sepphoris. From the tone of his comments after he had grown up and become a wandering prophet, it is evident he had not been brought up to have much respect for Herod.

At the same time as the revolt against Archelaus in Jerusalem, there had been a violent uprising in Galilee against the joint rule of Herod and of Rome. It was occasioned by a general census taken for tax purposes. That revolt was led by a Zealot from the city of Gamala called Judas of Galilee.

Raising the battle cry "No ruler but God," Judas called upon Jews of Galilee to make rebellion the sign of their commitment to their god. He was hailed by many Galileans as a messiah who would deliver them from foreign bondage. He came to Nazareth to exhort members of the synagogue of Joseph and Jesus to join his fanatical horde, and many of them did. Joseph and Jesus heard him, no doubt, but they would not have been among the ones who believed he was the messiah, because they already had other ideas on that subject.

Judas left Nazareth, and some days later he led a great mob of followers up to Sepphoris, where the people joyfully threw its gates open to him. He equipped all his followers with weapons and military stores they found in the armory of Herod Antipas there. Under Judas's direction the rebels improved the defenses of the city, and he led his men in prayers to their god to preserve them and the city during the Roman siege that would surely ensue.

While Jesus, Mary, and Joseph were wondering how that uprising would turn out, Herod Antipas sent an appeal to Varus to put down the insurrection. Varus brought his army, and after the inevitably successful Roman siege of Sepphoris and the slaughter of the rebel garrison, the city was destroyed. Varus did that in retribution for the support given to Judas by its inhabitants, whom he forced to dismantle all its great buildings, leaving not one stone upon another. The soldiers then burned all the wooden structures, and the people of that ruined city were chained and led away into slavery. That punishment was imposed upon them as a deterrent to future rebellion of the Galileans. Jews are permitted to own slaves, but they have a powerful aversion to being enslaved themselves. That disinclination is, I suppose, derived at least in part from their exalted view of themselves as the chosen people of their god.

The people of Nazareth and other nearby towns still mourn for their lost friends and former neighbors. Widows can still be heard there chanting prayers for husbands who joined Judas and were put to the sword in Sepphoris after it fell, and the children of those men join their mothers in reciting such prayers to their god, and Jesus would have heard that wailing every day. The residents of Nazareth still hope for divine deliverance from Roman rule, I am sure, but very few of them believe a prudent way of securing the kingdom of their god is to invite such another disaster.

As a youth, Jesus witnessed all the disturbing events of that time. From his father's carpenter shop he saw the brass-and-iron-bound legions of Rome passing by on their way to destroy the city he knew so well. Those soldiers were coming and going in Nazareth throughout the siege. They were stern and implacable veterans, the kind of men who would stamp a lasting impression on a young mind. In the street outside the door of the shop, Jesus would also have beheld the distraught people of Sepphoris—men, women, and children—as they were driven away into slavery from their ruined city. Not even the star of Bethlehem could have been more in the minds of the family of Joseph the carpenter than the fate of their chained and wailing countrymen who were marched by in the street day after day.

Ten years after the destruction of Sepphoris, Herod Antipas undertook to restore it on a scale more grand and beautiful than before. This reconstruction commenced after Jesus had grown to manhood but during the time he was still working at his trade. As a skilled carpenter who lived within walking distance of Sepphoris, he probably was employed there in the rebuilding of the city, but even if he was not, he surely must have gone up there from time to time and witnessed all the stages of reconstruction. By that great project of Herod Antipas, he would have been reminded throughout his youth of how his family's friends and neighbors had accepted the claims of Judas of Galilee that he was their promised messiah and of how those friends and neighbors had paid an awful price for their credulity.

I believe the destruction of the city of Sepphoris influenced the views of Jesus of Nazareth upon Roman rule of Palestine. Again and again toward the end of his life he indicated he understood the futility of rebellion.

It was during the time of the reconstruction of Sepphoris that Caesar Augustus died. The entire Roman world mourned the passing of the god who had governed it so well for half a century, bringing order and prosperity and peace out of what had been such a terrible series of civil wars. Like everyone else, the Jews approved of his words to the friends who had gathered around his deathbed at Nola: "Since I have played my part very well, clap your hands, and with applause dismiss me from the stage."

The people of Nazareth certainly did not want to be ruled by a Roman emperor, but they were willing to applaud the memory of Augustus in appreciation for the privileges he and his great-uncle had conferred upon them. Young men like Jesus and older men like Joseph were concerned about the future. They feared that the government of Tiberius, a grim old warrior, would not be so favorably disposed toward them.

With one exception there appears to be nothing preserved in the way of anecdotes about the childhood or the youth of Jesus. That one story is about an unusual episode at the very end of his childhood. When he was twelve years of age, on the threshold of manhood according to Jewish custom, Joseph and Mary took him to Jerusalem for a festival the Jews call Passover. This is a high holiday marked by the ritual consumption of unleavened bread and lambs that have been sacrificed on the altar in their temple. This rather dull sort of feast commemorates the deliverance of the Jews from slavery in Egypt in the time of Moses. Over that evening meal they recount with satisfaction some horrendous things they believe their god did to the Egyptians on their behalf to effect their liberation. While at the Passover table they also anticipate all the blessings that will accompany the advent of their messiah. Those singular rites bring hordes of Jewish pilgrims to Jerusalem from every part of the Roman Empire.

Jews are expressly commanded to rejoice at their religious festivals. Yet that commandment always seemed to me like an order of a centurion to his soldiers to enjoy themselves in spite of being in an unpleasant situation. Like all the other Jewish feasts, Passover would seem to Romans a rather glum affair. It is entirely given over to solemn prayers and sober worship. The feasting in which the Jews participate upon special occasions is not done for the pleasure of it. Feasting is just another of their solemn rituals.

They have no riotous deities like Bacchus and no amorous ones like Jupiter, and that one grim, invisible god they do have makes them painfully serious at every season of the year. They have no religious carnivals when a man can forget his troubles, no holidays when anyone can eat and drink to his heart's content and enjoy any woman—or man—who takes his fancy. More than once when we were there in Judea, I said to my wife, "If those bearded puritans could just loosen up and enjoy one good Saturnalia, it would diminish the problems they present to me and to everyone else."

She responded as if she were scandalized by that remark, and she probably was.

Joseph and Mary were part of a large company of people when they left Jerusalem on the road home to Galilee after the close of Passover. Their boy had not come with the party, as they had every reason to expect he would, but they were not aware of that because there was such a throng of travelers on the road. It was not until the end of the first day's journey that they became concerned about him. They sought him everywhere among their encamped friends but without success, and they became alarmed.

The next morning they returned to the city. After looking all around Jerusalem, they found the young fellow in one of the courts of the temple. He was seated among the learned men there as if he were one of them. He was gravely listening to them and asking them questions and even offering opinions of his own to them.

His mother said to him, "Why have you done this? Didn't you know your father and I would be worried about you?"

His response to that was, "Don't you know I must be about my father's business?"

That reply must have impressed the woman. It was a clear sign that the stories she and Joseph had told Jesus about his birth had been having a profound effect upon him.

In that year a powerful leader of the Sadducees named Annas was the high priest of the Jews. Either he or some other member of his family has filled that office throughout most of the half century since then. Caiaphas was his son-in-law. Annas himself played a role in the process that led to the execution of Jesus more than twenty years later. I have wondered whether Annas was among those who talked to him in the temple that day and whether the old man remembered that serious young fellow when Jesus was brought to his house for interrogation on the night before he died on his cross.

THREE

A Wayside Prophet

As far as I know, Jesus of Nazareth worked at his trade until he was thirty years of age. For some of that time he may have been employed as one of the workmen who rebuilt Sepphoris. Before that project commenced, he must have spent his days in Joseph's shop in Nazareth making chairs and tables and carts and plows and yokes for oxen, as carpenters do to earn their daily bread. Today Christians point out that this too corresponds with prophecies in old Jewish writings, ones which declare the messiah would live out most of his life in humble circumstances.

One day he was a carpenter. The next day he was a prophet. On that all agree. He put down his tools and left the shop of his reputed father and walked out of Nazareth in the year after my wife and I arrived in Palestine. He was then no concern of mine, since he went to join his cousin John the Baptist on the east bank of the Jordan River.

By that time John was an itinerant preacher in Perea. He had gone there after having stirred up a lot of hostility in Judea by publicly denouncing Pharisees and Sadducees alike as sanctimonious hypocrites. By all accounts, John was a genuine Jewish curiosity. Wearing a camel's-hair cloak and a wide leather belt, he appeared out of the desert, where he had been subsisting upon a diet of wild honey and grasshoppers. Before and after such delightful repasts, John denounced Pharisees and Sadducees and evil in high places, and he began calling on Jews to be baptized in the Jordan River as an indication of repentance for their sins.

Being unkempt from head to foot and wearing a long beard and longer hair, he appeared to be just another holy maniac, but many ordinary Jews began to think John was a new prophet of their god. Some of his followers were sure he was himself the messiah, and they tried to convince everyone else of that belief.

While John was still preaching in Judea, I sent an agent to hear him. My man came back to me the next day and told me there were Sadducees as well as Pharisees in the crowd that listened to him. John pointed them out and excoriated them as a generation of vipers. Soon after that he wisely departed for Perea on the far side of the Jordan River, because he would be out from under the jurisdiction of the Great Sanhedrin there.

When John went into Perea, Herod Antipas had his agents begin to keep track of him. Herod, as I have pointed out already, was beguiled by Greek philosophy, and that made him more tolerant of religious eccentrics than were most Jews. He was not of a mind to take action against anyone for defying the religious hierarchy. On the other hand, Herod did think it prudent to keep track of anyone in his realm who might eventually decide he was the messiah and raise a rebellion.

John caused great excitement among Jews by declaring that the Roman Empire and the rights of the Herodian lines of royalty would all be set aside in a new kingdom to be established by the Jewish god. He proclaimed himself the herald of the new king in ringing phrases. He declared, "I am the voice of one crying in the wilderness, prepare ye the way of the Lord."

John was not a political activist like Judas of Galilee, but his powerful diatribes were stirring up unrest among the people of Galilee and Perea. Every day he railed against evil in high places and, in doing so, he did not spare Herod Antipas. He denounced the

dance for Herod and then to implore him to give her John's head as a reward.

To casual observers it seemed the carpenter was just another of John's disciples, distinguishable from the rest only because he happened to be John's cousin. However, that perception changed when Jesus presented himself to John for baptism in the Jordan River and John protested, "It is I who should be baptized by you."

One of the strangest stories about Jesus has to do with his baptism by John. It is to the effect that as the carpenter was emerging from the river, the spirit of the Jewish god appeared in the form of a dove over him and said, "This is my son, in whom I am well pleased."

Like the legend of the angels appearing in the skies at the scene of his birth, this tale is believed by Christians and by no one else. Obviously, if such accounts had been given credence by very many Jews, the life story of Jesus of Nazareth would have had a different end. He might still be alive, and the worship of the Jewish god might have been changed by his survival.

Be that as it may, John repeatedly said that his cousin from Nazareth was the messiah whose appearance he had been told by their god to proclaim. As I reported in the previous chapter, Elizabeth, the mother of John, had accepted Jesus as the messiah before he

was born. Presumably, John had been brought up in that belief, just as Jesus himself had been. On one occasion when his cousin was among his listeners, John said of him, "Behold the lamb of God who takes away the sins of the world." In that declaration John was making reference to this passage from the Jewish writer named Isaiah: "The Lord laid upon him the iniquity of us all. . . . He is brought as a lamb to the slaughter."

John's allusion to Jesus being the lamb of God foreshadowed the course of the man's life. Jewish scriptures state that forgiveness of their sins by their god normally requires a blood sacrifice. The acceptance by Jesus of the role of sacrificial lamb—as ascribed to him by John—explains why he lived and died as he did.

Since John the Baptist did not consider Jesus of Nazareth to be just another disciple, the religious authorities did not either. In fact, most Jews took an interest in him when John declared he was the lord whose appearance he had come to foretell.

Soon after being baptized by John, Jesus returned to Galilee and took up residence in the city of Capernaum, a pleasant place on the northern shore of the Sea of Galilee. There he recruited a band of disciples, the majority of whom were fishermen and workmen from the area. At first he limited his ministry to the domain of Herod Antipas. Like John the Baptist, Jesus was aware that the tetrarch would be more tolerant of a self-styled prophet than the Great Sanhedrin in Jerusalem would ever be, so he began to wander around the green Galilean countryside, preaching to anyone who would listen. He appeared on the shores of the Sea of Galilee, he spoke on the hills and in the fields, he presented himself in the small towns, but he stayed out of the new city of Tiberias. Aside from the fact that it had been built on an old Jewish burial ground and was full of structures adorned with graven images, it was the usual residence of Herod and his wife and her dancing daughter. After the decapitation of his cousin John, Jesus probably wanted to show his disapproval of them by staying far away from them.

What is more, Tiberias has a mixed population, mostly Greeks and Syrians, because righteous Jews will not live in such a place. During those early months of his ministry, Jesus was appealing only to Jews. For that reason he was limiting his speaking appearances to places where the population was mostly Jewish. That is why he also stayed away from Sepphoris. Since its reconstruction it too was a place with a mixed lot of inhabitants.

The agents and informers of Herod were present in every crowd that gathered around the new wayside prophet in Galilee and Perea. They reported back to the tetrarch that the fellow was making quite an impression wherever he went. The Jews of Galilee often had been exhorted by other wandering preachers in recent years, but none of them had been anything like him. Before he spoke, he impressed his listeners with an ethereal self-assurance. Then he would move them with a very peculiar oratorical style. In all his sermons he spoke mysteriously, and I was told later by Herod that he was consciously complying with a phrase from the Jewish scriptures: "I will speak in parables. I will utter dark sayings of old."

Like almost all other religious agitators among the Jews, he concerned himself largely with the advent of the kingdom of their god. That impending earthly paradise, he taught, will involve the rule of the Jewish god in the hearts of all men. It will only be attained by discerning the will of that god and by demonstrating a faithful obedience to it in every way. Much of what he said was in accord with the teachings of the Pharisees, especially when he set forth what he considered to be the proper ways for men to deal with each other.

For example, he said, "Do unto others what you would have them do unto you." A few years earlier a leader of the Pharisees named Hillel had expressed the same thoroughly impractical sentiment in almost the same words: "What is hateful to you do not do to anyone else."

Jesus of Nazareth took that innocent strain of insanity even further. He admonished his followers to love their enemies, to do good to those who do them harm, to bless those who curse them, and to pray for those who persecute them. He once said, "Whoever shall strike you upon the right cheek, turn the other cheek to him. And if any man requires you to go a mile with him, go another mile with him."

The fact that a Roman soldier could require any man he met to carry his gear a mile had rankled in the hearts of Jews. To order them to voluntarily bear a Roman soldier's load an extra mile was to demand a preternatural level of submission. By making this sort of comment, the man indicated he was not a threat to the authority of Rome or of Herod Antipas. On the contrary, he was an advocate of compliance with it.

As I have already mentioned, Herod was maintaining a constant surveillance of the carpenter. Though Herod and I were then still at odds with each other, his agents passed information they gathered on to my people, who wanted to know what this wayside prophet was saying and doing in Galilee, because any potential messianic movement there could affect Jews in my jurisdiction whenever its leader decided to come into Judea or Samaria. However, the more I heard about the fellow, the more I was put at ease by other sayings that were being attributed to him. At one point, while preaching on a mountaintop, he said, "Blessed are the meek, for they shall inherit the earth." In that same sermon he said, "Blessed are the peacemakers, for they shall be called the children of God" and "Blessed are the merciful, for they shall obtain mercy." He made other statements in harmony with those, all of which made it seem to me in the best interests of Rome to be sure nothing bad happened to the fellow.

At that time I had a Jewish scribe working for me. The man was the second son of a family who had recently been wine merchants but had lost everything when two ships that were laden in part with their cargoes foundered in a great storm.

One afternoon I asked him, "Why does this carpenter stir up the Pharisees so much?"

He replied, "The Scriptures and the Law are normally explained to the people by rabbis who have spent years earning the right to teach, so it's an offense to them that he puts himself on a level above them. And they're upset by how he's interpreting the law."

"What do you mean?"

"He's telling people they don't have to be so scrupulous about complying with our religious codes, and that infuriates the Pharisees. And they are wrought up because he is decreeing impossible standards of righteousness for human conduct. He says any man who lusts after any woman who isn't his wife has committed adultery in his heart."

I laughed when I heard that.

"Why do you laugh?" the scribe said.

"Above all of our other gods, we Romans venerate Jupiter, who jumps in and out of women's beds, begetting illegitimate offspring, and most of us do our best to follow the example he sets for us. Why shouldn't we be amused by any such unnatural rules for human conduct?"

"Our God is different," the scribe said.

"That is unfortunate for you," I responded. "Now tell me why the successful Jews I know all hate that carpenter."

"He told one rich man, 'You must give away all you own if you want to be virtuous.' To another he said, 'A man cannot serve God and Mammon.' To yet another he said, 'It is easier for a camel to pass through the eye of a needle than for a rich man to enter the kingdom of God.'"

"Those are radical doctrines."

"They are considered subversive by every Jew who owns a farm or a business."

"Comments like those can make him a lot of enemies," I said.

"He's gaining enemies—and supporters—every day. Yesterday I got a letter from my older brother, who now lives in Capernaum, and in it he says that the carpenter is becoming famous as a worker of miracles. At a big wedding in the town of Cana he turned some water into wine, and he is supposed to be curing people of leprosy, palsy, dropsy, madness, lameness, blindness, and deafness."

At that point my chief assistant came into my chamber. With a wink of one eye, I told him, "Joel has gotten a letter from his brother that says the carpenter has been curing the blind and the deaf and the lame and the mad in Galilee."

My chief assistant responded cheerfully, "It's always easy to find accomplices who'll pretend to be blind or deaf or lame or mad and who'll pretend to recover at the appropriate time, if you give them enough money to make it worth their while."

"It's a practice as old as mankind," I replied.

"A lot of people only think they are sick," my chief assistant said, "and a fellow like that carpenter can persuade them they've suddenly gotten better."

"True," I replied with another wink at him. "Cynics have been saying the same thing about the cures at the shrines of Aesculapius for centuries, and they may be right too."

My scribe broke in with, "My brother says he's seen Jesus cure lepers, so he's doing more than just talking people out of imagined sicknesses."

"Maybe your brother is telling the truth," my chief assistant said, "and maybe he isn't."

That upset my scribe. He said, "Jews are coming from all over Perea and Galilee to Jesus. They are bringing their sick relatives and friends to be cured by him."

"So I've heard," my chief assistant said with a smile. "Maybe I should go to him with my hernia."

He left the room and so did my scribe, and I reflected on the fact that the carpenter was attracting more and more attention as a very holy man. Among the Jews the power to heal has always been considered a mark of godly authority. In that they are like other peoples. As we all know, the veneration of Aesculapius by Greeks and Romans arises out of all those heaps of crutches that have been piled up around his shrine at Epidaurus over hundreds of years by lame people who have walked away cured.

One morning my scribe told me, "Yesterday I got another letter from my brother in Galilee, and in it he says he heard from various people that the carpenter is supposed to have walked on the surface of the water of the Sea of Galilee."

"Do people actually believe such things?" I said.

"They also believe he commanded a storm to stop and it did."

"He should sell that service to shipowners," my chief assistant replied.

A week later my scribe told me, "I got another letter from my brother yesterday."

"He writes to you pretty often."

"He wants me to know about the carpenter. He says everybody is talking about how he brought two dead people back to life. One of them was the daughter of a rich man named Jairus, and the other was the son of a widow in the city of Nain."

I responded, "Why should I pay attention to such stories?"

"Because resurrections of the dead are supposed to accompany the advent of the Messiah."

Two weeks later the man told me about another alleged miracle. "My brother went with a multitude of people to hear the carpenter preach on the western shore of the Sea of Galilee," he said, "and after the man stopped speaking, he fed that whole crowd with a few loaves and fishes that had been brought by one boy."

My chief assistant came into my chamber in time to hear that. He said, "Probably a lot of people in that crowd had brought loaves and fishes but had kept them concealed for fear of being asked to share them by people who had nothing to eat, so when the carpenter started to divide up the boy's lunch, they were shamed into adding theirs to the common store."

"If that was the case," I said, "the miracle was just as real. Getting those tight-fisted Galileans to share what they had brought for themselves was amazing."

The scribe looked unhappy. "That crowd tried to crown him then and there," he said, "but he wouldn't let them."

My chief assistant snickered and said, "Those Jews have been waiting for a messiah who will identify himself to them by working wonders. And when this fellow provided them with some lunch, they thought he had revealed himself to them."

Before long that erstwhile carpenter was calling himself the Son of Man, and his assumption of that title, which had been used by their prophet Daniel for the coming messiah, created a great stir among the Jews.

One morning while I was at my desk in the palace of Herod the Great and going over some documents relating to a building project, a Jewish priest appeared before me. "I have a letter for you from the high priest," he said, and he handed me a roll of papyrus. It became an important item among my records that related to Jesus of Nazareth, and I recovered it today from the room where I store my old documents. Here it is:

To Pontius Pilate,
Procurator of the provinces of Judea, Samaria, and
Idumea:
Peace be unto you.

As high priest of the Jews, I have been told a lot of
stories about that carpenter who is taking tremendous
honors upon himself. If the miracles he is being credited
with are genuine, they may be evidence of divine authority
granted to him. If they are not, they may be
manifestations of an evil, instead of a divine, power. In
either case, I am obliged to pay attention to him.

As you well know, heresy is a capital crime among
Jews and is punishable by death. In that connection, there
is mention in our law that a false prophet is a preacher of
apostasy who will try to lead Israel astray through magic
and deception of the senses, as well as by genuine
miracles. Such a false prophet is possessed by the great
evil spirit who is the enemy of our God. This devil we call
Satan, and the wonders a false prophet performs are
accomplished through powers granted to him by Satan. If
a man is judged to be a false prophet by the Great
Sanhedrin, he is to be sentenced to death by stoning. As
the presiding officer of that court, I sent agents to Galilee
to investigate the miracles performed there by that
carpenter. They concluded that the cures and exorcisms
and other wonders he performed were authentic. The
question I must now decide is the critical one. By whose
authority are those miracles done? Is that carpenter a

man of God, or is he a deceiver who will try to lead us all
to our destruction?

Scribes and Pharisees have also gone to Galilee to
listen to the carpenter and to observe all he is doing. They
were disturbed when they saw him enter the homes of
publicans and other nefarious Jews to eat and drink with
them. Scribes and Pharisees, of course, are never willing
to dine with anybody who is not one of themselves, for fear
any other host might not have the same knowledge of the
Law and the same regard for it as they do themselves.
Therefore they thought Jesus was not showing the concern
he should to avoid being defiled. That man would even sit
down and eat and drink at the tables of impious men at
times when religious Jews should be fasting. Critics called
him to task for that, and he said to them, "I have come to
call sinners to repentance, not the righteous."

The scribes and Pharisees were even more upset when
they saw some of his disciples eating with unwashed
hands. They asked him, "Why don't your disciples live
according to the traditions of the elders? Instead they eat
with their hands defiled."

This was a serious violation of our law, and in his
answer the fellow directly challenged that law. "You
hypocrites," he shouted at them, "Isaiah said of you,
'These men honor me with their lips but not their hearts.'
You lay aside the commandments of God and observe
traditions of men that have to do with the washing of pots
and pans. And by doing so, you make the word of God of
no effect." Later, to his disciples, he added to that impious

reply, "There is nothing outside a man which by going into him can defile him, since it enters not his heart but his stomach and passes on. What comes out of a man is what defiles him. From within, from the heart of a man, come evil thoughts, adulteries, murders, thefts, pride, and foolishness."

This commentary was repeated by his disciples as illustrating his wisdom, so it reached the ears of the scribes and the Pharisees who were keeping him under surveillance. By those words he implied that all food is ritually clean and fit to eat, a horrifying heresy to Pharisees and Sadducees alike.

He also appalled my representatives, as well as the Pharisees and scribes who were present, when he cured a paralytic man and said to him, "Your sins are forgiven you."

In response all the Pharisees there properly declared, "This man speaks blasphemies. No one can forgive sin but God himself."

On the basis of such reports from my agents, I have concluded the man is an apostate.

In your next dispatch to the Emperor, please assure him that the priests of Israel pray daily for his well-being.

With all due respects,
Joseph ben Caiaphas

At about that time some members of the carpenter's family came to the conclusion that he was out of his mind and should be locked up for his own sake, before some of the religious leaders undertook to deal with him. However, his relatives failed in their attempts to abduct him, so the tragedy of his life was acted out eventually to the very end they feared.

Jesus soon put himself into conflict with the highest Jewish authorities over another of their most important religious customs, the observance of the sabbath day. He was taken to task by scribes and Pharisees because some of his disciples plucked kernels of corn to eat upon the sabbath, breaking the law against reaping on that day. Also he healed people on the sabbath, one man with a withered arm and one with dropsy. These cures were in violation of the law, which prohibits a physician from treating a patient on the sabbath unless the person's life is in danger. The setting of a fractured limb is forbidden, for example, by that stern code.

When some Pharisees charged Jesus with a lack of respect for the sabbath, he replied, "The Son of Man is lord even of the sabbath." By this reply also he set himself above the sacred law of Moses.

This kind of direct challenge from a man who was attracting so many followers alarmed all the religious authorities, scribes, rabbis, and priests alike. One of the most cherished hopes of all devout Jews is to become worthy of this promise Moses said their god had made to them through him: "You shall keep my sabbath and reverence my sanctuary. If you walk in accord with my statutes and you keep my commandments, you will chase your enemies and they will fall before you. Five of you shall chase a hundred, and a hundred of you shall put ten thousand to flight."

You can imagine who they have in mind.

For a couple of weeks my Jewish scribe did not mention receiving any more news from Galilee. Then one morning he told me, "I got a long letter from my brother yesterday."

"I suppose it's another one about the carpenter," I said.

"Yes. He's continuing to enrage the Pharisees."

"He seems to be making a career of it."

"Now he's criticizing them for praying too loud and too often in public places."

"Whenever I hear any of them doing that on a street corner," I said, "I think it's too obvious a display of godlessness."

"All Pharisees aren't guilty of that," the man replied. "They themselves are willing to admit there are hypocrites among them, but they are outraged at what the carpenter is doing. He is implying that all Pharisees are hypocrites."

"What does your brother think about that?"

"He believes that what Jesus is saying needs to be said, but he's worried about the effect his attacks will have on the Pharisees."

"They will agree with Caiaphas that the man is a sorcerer," I said.

"They already have done that," the scribe replied. "They have declared that his miracles are manifestations of the power of the devil."

"Doesn't the carpenter see the danger to himself in that?"

"Who knows?" The scribe shook his head profoundly. "He keeps coming up with new ways to shock them. My brother mentions in his letter that Jesus has said, 'I am the light of the world.' And he did it where scribes and Pharisees could hear him."

It is not at all surprising that some devout Jews attempted to kill Jesus as an apostate. One sabbath day, after he had delivered a commentary upon a scriptural passage in his own synagogue in the town of Nazareth, members of the congregation, many of whom had known him since childhood, tried to throw him off a cliff nearby, but he escaped from them.

It was becoming clear to me that—mad or sane—he knew what he was doing and understood what the consequences would inevitably be for him. During that summer in Galilee he often predicted that he would be crucified in Jerusalem. More than once he said to his followers, "If any man will come after me, let him deny himself and take up his cross and follow me."

That quotation is taken directly from a written report I have before me now. An agent of Herod Antipas sent it to me. He wanted me to be aware the carpenter was saying I would kill him—because I was the only person in Judea who could order that punishment for anyone. I was puzzled by that prediction because it implied he was planning to raise a rebellion that would fail, and that seemed a strange thing for him to prophesy.

The themes of his sermons were becoming increasingly mystical. A quotation from one of them is in the report I have before me now. It reads, "The Son of Man must suffer many things and be rejected by the high priests and the scribes, and be killed, and after three days rise again."

I sent my copy of the report to Caiaphas without comment.

He sent it back to me the same day with a note on the bottom of it in his own bold handwriting. I can still read it easily in spite of the dimness of my sight. It says, "I received a similar account from my representatives in Galilee. What the carpenter is now saying about rising from the dead after three days is much too reminiscent of the Babylonian belief in Tammuz.

By choosing three days as the duration of his predicted stay in the tomb, that fellow is challenging us to deal with him."

Early in the fall of the year, Jesus of Nazareth informed his followers in Galilee that he was going to Jerusalem. Then he set forth with twelve of his disciples on the road to that city where he had often predicted he would be tried and executed for heresy.

So it was that he came into my jurisdiction.

FOUR

No One Ever Spoke Like Him

*J*esus walked into Jerusalem with his disciples in time for a Jewish harvest festival called the Feast of the Tabernacles. He came through the east gate of the city early in the afternoon of a clear fall day. His arrival caused tremendous excitement among the throngs of pilgrims who were crowding the city. As he passed among those people, many of them were hailing him as the messiah, and others were cursing him as a heretic.

I spent all that afternoon in the palace of Herod the Great, playing host to the vain young son of Vitellius, who had come to the Near East to tour his father's new dominions. After we took off our togas to get into Herod's enormous bath, the young fellow struck a pose to show off his naked body to me, and he said, "You know, I wouldn't agree to get into bed with the Emperor until he promised to give Father the post of president of Syria."

"Is that what your father wanted you to do?" I asked him.

"It was his idea," he replied.

Just as we sat down on the edge of the bath to lower our legs into the hot water, an elderly manservant came into the room and said to me, "That carpenter has just come into the city."

"So I've heard," I replied. "Go and follow him and report to me everything he says and does today."

As the servant left us, young Vitellius slipped into the water and said, "Why are you interested in carpenters?"

"This one is unusual," I told him as I slid into the bath.

That night I had dinner alone with Vitellius, and when we had finished eating, that old manservant appeared to make his report. He bowed to us both. "I found that carpenter in the forecourt of the temple," he declared. "He'd gone there with his disciples and was preaching to a crowd of Jews."

"What is this carpenter like?" Vitellius asked.

"He is a handsome man with a beautiful speaking voice," my servant replied very solemnly.

"Is he as handsome as I am?" Vitellius inquired.

"What was he saying?" I asked the servant.

"One of the things he said was, 'Some of you who stand here will not taste of death until you have seen the kingdom of god in all its glory.'"

"He's mad," Vitellius said.

"What else did he say?" I asked the man.

"'Anyone who saves his life will lose it, but anyone who loses his life for my sake shall live forever.'"

"Why are we talking about that crazy man?" Vitellius sighed. "Let's talk about me. A Spanish soothsayer once told me I'll be the emperor someday."

To my manservant I said, "I want you to follow the carpenter each day. Act as if you're one of his admirers."

Young Vitellius left the next day to return to his father in Antioch. Now, thirty years later, he no longer has to sleep with great men, because he is a great man himself, and the idea that he will become emperor no longer seems so unlikely.

The next evening my old manservant came back to report to me while my wife and I were lying on our couches after a good supper. He bowed to us each and said, "Today that man was preaching to some Jews in a forecourt of the temple, and a group of Pharisees dragged a woman before him. She was struggling and screaming and cursing at them. The carpenter stopped talking, and one of the Pharisees said to him, 'We found this woman in the act of committing adultery with a man,' and she kept yelling, 'Make them let me go!' Another Pharisee said, 'The law of Moses commands that any woman taken in adultery must be stoned. What do you say?'"

"And what did he say?" my wife asked the man.

"What could he say?" the man answered her. "If he told them she should be stoned, they would have done it then and there, and he would have been guilty of inciting them to kill her, and that would have been murder under Roman law."

"It certainly would," I commented.

"But if he said she should not be stoned, they would tell everyone he had contradicted the word of their god."

"So what did he do?" my wife inquired.

"He stooped and wrote in the dust with one finger, 'Gluttony, lust, rage, envy, and sloth.'"

"Those are things the Jews consider wicked," I told my wife.

The servant went on, "Then the carpenter stood up and said, 'Let him who is without sin cast the first stone.' He stared at one after another of the Pharisees in the crowd, and they stared back at him. One by one those men drifted away. At last there was no one left around him but his followers and the woman. He told her, 'Go and sin no more,' and she went away shouting, 'Jesus of Nazareth is a great man!'"

The servant left us, and my wife said, "If they don't punish men for adultery, they shouldn't kill women for it."

I replied, "Oh, my dear Claudia, do be sensible."

"I think that carpenter is a good person," she said.

"That may be, but those Pharisees who accused that woman will never forgive him for making them look foolish."

The next night my servant came and told us, "He was preaching in the forecourt of the temple again today, and I overheard one of his listeners say, 'Isn't this the man they seek to kill? Yet here he is speaking openly, and they say nothing to him,' and another one said, 'Can it be they know he is the messiah?' A few minutes after that some temple guards marched onto the scene. They had been sent by the chief priests to seize the carpenter, but those men made the mistake of listening to him before arresting him, and they said to each other, 'No one ever spoke like this man.' And they went away without arresting him."

"He must be very impressive," my wife said.

"His voice is the voice of a great man," the servant replied. "For hours on end he raises it over the bellowing and bleating of the animals that are to be sacrificed on the altar, and nobody ever has any trouble hearing him. And he has the manner of a great man. Today he said, 'I am the light of the world.' His followers were all impressed by that."

"That's too bad," I said. "He's quite mad, and it would be a good thing for him if people did laugh at him."

The next night, my man informed us, "Today the carpenter told some Pharisees, 'You are of your father the devil, and the lusts of your father you will do. He who is of God hears God's words. You don't hear them because you are not of God.'"

"They must have hated that," my wife said.

"They shouted at him, 'You are possessed by a devil!' and he replied, 'If a man obeys my words, he will not die.' One of the Pharisees scoffed, 'Abraham is dead, and you say that if any man obeys your words, he will never die. Are you greater than Abraham who is dead? Who do you make yourself out to be?' and that mad carpenter said, 'Your father Abraham rejoiced to see my day, and he has seen it, and is glad.' An older Pharisee answered him, 'You are not fifty years old, and have you seen Abraham?' and he cried, 'Before Abraham was, I am!' One of the younger Pharisees shouted, 'Did you hear him? This fellow is telling us he is God!' Then all the Pharisees picked up rocks and threw them at him."

"Were they trying to kill him?" I asked.

"Yes, they were, but he covered his head with his arms, and his followers led him away."

"I'm glad he got away," my wife said.

My man told us the following night, "When the carpenter came to preach in the temple today, his nose was swollen and cut, and one of his cheeks was black and blue. As soon as a crowd gathered around him, he said, 'I and the Father are one.' Some Pharisees and some scribes who were there began to throw stones at him, and his followers gathered around him again and hurried him away."

The Great Sanhedrin decided the time had come for an official investigation into the culpability of the man. They called upon a Jew who had been blind from birth, or so he said. This man had made his living as a beggar at one of the gates of Jerusalem. At the time they called him as a witness, he could see. He said he had been cured of his blindness by the carpenter. The alleged cure had taken place on the previous sabbath day.

The proceedings of the Great Sanhedrin are public, so I sent my old manservant to observe the hearing.

That night he came to tell me and my wife what had happened. He said, "The old high priest, Annas, started things off by saying to the beggar, 'I don't think you were ever blind. I think you've been putting on an act for all these years at the city gate because you're too idle to make a living by honest work.' Then a younger priest who was sitting next to Annas said, 'That carpenter is not from God, because he does not keep the Sabbath.'"

"And what did the beggar say to that?" my wife asked.

"He said, 'That man is surely a prophet. God does not listen to sinners, but if anyone is a worshiper of God and does his will, God will listen to him. If this man were not from God, he could do nothing.' And then Joseph ben Caiaphas said, 'The carpenter is a heretic, and this man should be excommunicated for what he just said.' All seventy members of that council cried, 'Yes!' and the beggar was excommunicated."

For a brief time the man from Nazareth continued to move about in Judea. He kept creating further problems for himself by healing people wherever he went. He also kept saying things like, "I and the Father are one."

Some Pharisees and scribes stoned him in the city of Lydda. Again he was injured, but he again escaped with his life. After that he departed from Judea and led his apostles beyond the Jordan River into Perea.

When I told my wife of his departure, she asked me, "Will he be safe there?"

"Yes," I told her. "He will. Herod made enough trouble for himself by executing John the Baptist. He won't want to kill this fellow."

Jesus preached to crowds there in Perea. Certain Pharisees, apparently thinking they could create problems for him with Herod similar to those that had proved fatal to John the Baptist, posed this question to him one day: "Is it lawful for a man to put away his wife?" They were raising an issue concerning the law of Moses that allows divorce. I am sure they knew he had expressed himself on the subject in the past and that he concurred with more recent Jewish authorities who disapprove of divorce.

He answered them, "Any man who puts away his wife and then marries another commits adultery."

The Pharisees sent word to Herod about what he had said. The tetrarch felt no need to respond. In the matter of his divorce he was content to rest upon the authority of Moses, and his wife was not disposed to get Herod to behead his subjects for condemning divorce, as long as they didn't mention hers specifically.

Some of the Pharisees, who presumably wanted to get Jesus back into Judea, where he would be subject to the authority of the Great Sanhedrin, went to him and told him he should flee because Herod sought to take his life.

His answer conveyed to all who heard it his low opinion of the tetrarch. He said, "Go and tell that fox it cannot be that a prophet should perish out of Jerusalem."

Jesus knew that remark would get back to the tetrarch, and by it he again showed he thought he was in no danger from Herod. In that same statement, though, he was saying that when he returned to Jerusalem, it would be to go to his grave.

Then an event occurred which set everything in motion toward the grim death Jesus had so often predicted for himself. While he lingered beyond the Jordan River in Perea, a friend of his named Lazarus fell ill. The carpenter had often stayed with this man and his two sisters, who lived in a little town called Bethany. This village is on the southeastern side of a hill called the Mount of Olives, which rises just to the east of Jerusalem. The sisters of Lazarus, whose names were Mary and Martha, sent word to Jesus of the illness of their brother, and they implored him to come and heal Lazarus.

Jesus hesitated in Perea, perhaps out of a reasonable aversion to leaving this world himself. When he at last set foot on the road to Bethany, Lazarus had been in his tomb for four days.

Among the small company that followed the carpenter on that journey was one of my Jewish agents. The man reported to me that the sister of Lazarus whose name was Martha met Jesus on the road just outside Bethany and said to him, "If you had been here, my brother would not have died." When he entered the town, Mary also came to him and told him the same thing. Jesus went to the cave where Lazarus had been interred, and called upon him to come forth. And he did!

The next day I received the following letter from Caiaphas.

To Pontius Pilate,
Procurator of the provinces of Judea, Samaria, and
Idumea:
Peace be unto you.

By the time you receive this letter, you will have heard the carpenter has allegedly raised a friend of his named Lazarus from the dead. I presume that theatrical performance was an elaborately staged hoax, although it's also possible Lazarus was in a catatonic state and was awakened by the heretic. In either case the result was the same. Most of the people of Jerusalem have accepted the resurrection of Lazarus as genuine, and that also is a possibility. A lot of Pharisees see in it the most decisive proof yet that Jesus of Nazareth is an evil sorcerer.

His followers have of course hailed the raising of Lazarus as a miracle accomplished by the power of our God, and the entire city of Jerusalem is in a turmoil of disputes. The resurrection of dead people is supposed to be a sign of the advent of a messiah, and a furor arose when some time ago in Galilee the carpenter revived two young people who appeared to be dead. With the appearance of Lazarus from his tomb, that mad hysteria has become intensified. Jews have been waiting all their lives for a worker of wonders, and many of them think he has come at last.

Jewish cooperation with Rome is the only way to preserve our people in our land, as I have often declared publicly. Now I am concerned that the mobs in Jerusalem might become uncontrollable. You must have heard that a throng in Galilee offered Jesus a crown after he had fed them some bread and fish. He refused it then, but now he has said, "I and the Father are one," and that may be taken as a claim that he is the messiah.

I am afraid the insane enthusiasm of the mob for him may set the wheels of rebellion in motion again. I shudder when I remember the crosses that were raised by Varus outside the walls of Jerusalem in the course of the last general insurrection here. I am also appalled by the tragic outcome of the rebellion raised by Judas of Galilee. And I am horrified by the thought that Rome will tolerate only a limited number of such insurrections before it decides that such an intractable people must be dispossessed of their land and dispersed. That is what the king of Assyria decided long ago, when he scattered the ten northern tribes of Israel all over his empire. God forbid that should happen to what is left of His chosen people.

I am writing this letter to let you know I am going to convene a council of chief priests and leading Pharisees to discuss how to deal with Jesus of Nazareth.

With all due respects,
Joseph ben Caiaphas

The day after I received that letter, Caiaphas called upon the chief priests to meet in his palace, and he put this question to them: "What shall we do? This man seems to do miracles. If we leave him alone, the people will think he is the messiah, and then the Romans will come and take away our place and our nation." He was speaking to the political concerns of the Sadducees. The Pharisees were not present, because the meeting was a council of the chief priests. The Pharisees were concerned about Jesus only for spiritual reasons. If dealing with him had been left to them, they would have kept on asking him theological questions in public places, in the expectation one of his answers would discredit him with the majority of Jews sooner or later.

I should mention that, as the high priest of the Jews, Joseph ben Caiaphas was my appointee. In the time of Herod the Great, the king had been the one who appointed the high priest. On the death of Herod, Archelaus was left that power together with his realm of Judea, Samaria, and Idumea. When Archelaus was deposed by Caesar Augustus and replaced with a Roman governor, that power was passed on to the governor, and that was a sore point with the Jews. They thought they should be involved in the choice of their high priest. However, having the governor do it had substantial advantages for Rome. The term of office was only one year, so a governor could keep the spiritual leader of the Jews on a short leash. Caiaphas always supported me in all I did during my ten years in Palestine, so I reappointed him every year until I was replaced by Vitellius and arrested and sent back to Rome to be tried before the emperor.

Caiaphas said to the meeting he had convened, "It is expedient that one man should die for the people, that the nation should not perish." In response to that declaration, the priests and elders decided Jesus should be put to death. They issued a decree that any person who knew the whereabouts of the carpenter must reveal it in order that he might be arrested.

All during this time Jesus continued to tell his followers he would die on a cross in Jerusalem. This fixed idea of his harkened back to the declaration made by John the Baptist that he was the lamb of their god who had come to atone for the sins of the world through a blood sacrifice, and in the Jewish religion such blood sacrifices take place only in Jerusalem.

While he was predicting such a death for himself in Jerusalem, Jesus had his own ideas about when it should take place. For obvious symbolic reasons, he chose to defer it until Passover, when Jews take lambs to the temple to be sacrificed. Therefore he retreated into Samaria until that time had almost come.

Finally he turned his steps toward Jerusalem, leading his band of disciples there for the last time. When he got to the city, he led his followers through it on the way to Bethany. He had supper that evening in the home of Lazarus and his sisters.

When I told my wife he had come back to Jerusalem, she asked me, "What will happen to him now?"

I replied, "He apparently has it in mind that he is going to die here on a cross."

"But that is a Roman punishment for breaking Roman laws," she said. "Only you could condemn him to die that way."

"And he has broken no Roman laws," I replied. "At least not yet."

FIVE

Triumph and Despair

It was customary for the governor to stay in Jerusalem during the week of Passover. The city was always teeming then with pious pilgrims from all parts of the Middle East. The potential for an outburst of Jewish nationalist insanity was greater during religious festivals than at other times. Therefore I remained, with my wife, in Jerusalem, even though the weather was becoming unseasonably hot and my wife wanted to go down to Caesarea, where the cool breezes off the Mediterranean keep the days pleasant.

Each morning while we were in Jerusalem, a company of Syrian soldiers would march up to the front gates of the palace of Herod the Great, and they would serve as my bodyguard as I walked up the street to the Fortress Antonia, which was about eight hundred yards away. I performed my daily duties as governor in that great stone citadel, in a chamber which was up a wide flight of stairs. That room was a large square space furnished with one upright chair and an olivewood table that I used as a desk. In the stone wall opposite the door were two widely separated windows—narrow ones that opened out onto the street below so archers could shoot arrows from them if rebellious Jews ever seized the city again and besieged the fortress as they had done in times past.

In the afternoon of the first day of Passover week, I was up in that chamber listening to the officer in command of the garrison at the fortress tell me about the poor quality of some military stores he had received from Egypt. His voice was raised in exasperation, but I suddenly heard shouting and singing in the street outside.

"I wonder what that is all about," I said.

"Shall I send somebody to find out?" the officer asked me.

"That won't be necessary," I replied. "That noise is getting louder. The people making it are coming this way."

I went over to one of the narrow windows and looked out and saw a man riding into my line of sight on a gray donkey. He was tall and had dark brown hair, and he was wearing a robe woven out of fine white wool. Like most Jews, he wore his hair parted in the middle, and it came down to his shoulders. Also like most Jews, he had an untrimmed beard. His eyes were looking straight ahead as he rode his little steed down the street underneath my window, and his face, which was handsome and tan, looked very grave.

A hysterical mob of men and women who were swarming after him then filled the street. Many of them were shouting, "This is the prophet Jesus of Nazareth!" and others were crying, "Blessed is he who comes in the name of the Lord!" and "Hosannah, hosanna to the son of David!" A young woman was walking along behind the donkey and singing, "Hosannah! Hosannah! Hosannah!"

The garrison commander had gone to look out the other window, and he said, "There he is."

"He really is a fine-looking fellow," I commented. That was, of course, the first time I had ever seen him, and I was impressed with his lordly appearance and demeanor.

A few older men in the black costumes of Pharisees were among the crowd. One of those men looked up and saw me standing at my window watching that turbulent procession passing by. "Stop this!" he cried to the carpenter. "Tell all these people to stop this!"

Jesus of Nazareth rode on as if he had not heard that cry, and the mob following him kept on shouting madly, "Hosannah! Hosannah! Hosannah!"

The same Pharisee jostled his way through the chanting mob to the carpenter and tugged at his sleeve. "The governor will send soldiers out to kill these people," the Pharisee cried out. "Like he did to those Galileans in the temple."

"Shall I send my men out to do that?" the garrison commander asked me.

"No," I replied.

The Pharisees were all crying, "Stop this! Stop this!"

Without looking back at them, the carpenter replied in a loud, clear voice, "I tell you that if these people were silent, the very stones would cry out."

Over redoubled cries of "Hosannah!" from the crowd, I heard a knocking at the door of my chamber, and I said, "Come in."

The door opened and my chief assistant came through it. He said, "There is a messenger from Caiaphas here to see you."

As the carpenter passed out of sight down the street, I turned from the window.

A young Jew was coming into the room. He was wearing a plain brown robe, and I recognized him as a servant of the high priest.

"Peace be unto you," he said to me.

"And to you," I replied, and I motioned for my chief assistant and the commander of the garrison to leave the room.

As soon as the door closed behind them, the young man said to me, "A few hours ago some of the disciples of the carpenter came into the city and began to roam around the streets telling people that he was going to appear on the Mount of Olives this afternoon riding on a donkey and that he was going to come into Jerusalem on it. When the high priest heard that, he was very upset, and he told me to go out and observe everything that happened."

"Why should the appearance of the carpenter on a donkey upset the high priest?" I asked him.

"Because the prophet Zechariah wrote, 'Tell the daughters of Zion, behold, thy king cometh unto thee. He is just and having salvation, lowly and riding upon an ass, and upon a colt, the foal of an ass.'"

"And does his appearing on the Mount of Olives also have some special significance?" I asked.

"That is where the messiah is supposed to appear. By doing that, the fellow is declaring to all Jews that he is the messiah."

"And how did people respond to that?"

"They got very excited when they heard about it. Hundreds of them went out through the eastern gates of the city and down into the valley of the brook Kidron and on through the groves of olive trees and upward onto the mountain to greet the fellow. Many of those people were carrying palm fronds and holding them upright, as if they were welcoming royalty. They knelt down and laid their fronds across his path, and others began strewing their garments before him. He hardly paid any attention to them as he rode his donkey over their clothing, which finally became a long carpet that reached down the hill before him to the stone bridge that crosses the brook."

"Common people used to do things like that for Julius Caesar," I replied. "That's why Brutus and the others killed him."

My young visitor flinched as if I had insulted him. He then went on, "That multitude escorted the carpenter across the valley to the eastern gate of the city, shouting, "Hosannah!" and then followed him down the street past the guards in front of this fortress."

"I saw them go by," I said.

"The high priest wants you to understand what is happening. He says the fellow would not have ridden that donkey in from the Mount of Olives if he didn't intend to raise a rebellion."

"I want you to report to me whatever happens this evening."

"Of course," the young man said, and he left me.

The next morning the same young man came to me in my room at the fortress. As he passed through the door and approached me, he said, "The high priest told me to bring this to you." He reached forward to hand me a manuscript. It was the one about the birth of the carpenter that constitutes the first chapter of this book.

I accepted that roll of paper and said, "Tell me what happened after the carpenter rode by here on his donkey yesterday."

"He rode through the city and up to the temple," the young man replied dourly. "When he got there, he left his animal outside the gate and went into the forecourt of the temple, where he talked to those people who had been following him. He told them he is the son of God, and they all shouted, 'Hosannah! Hosannah! Hosannah in the highest!' After dark he left the temple with his disciples, and they walked out the east gate of the city and around the Mount of Olives to Bethany, where they spent the night."

"Make your future reports in writing," I told him. "I want to have a record of them."

In the morning of each day of that week I received from the same young man a written report of what the carpenter had said and done on the previous day. I kept those reports in case I might be called upon to defend my decisions with regard to the carpenter. I still have them, and they provide me with some of the details in the following account of the last few days of the man's life.

Halfway through the afternoon of the second day of the week, my chief assistant came to my chamber. "That carpenter has just come through the eastern gate of the city," he told me. "And he's on his way to the temple."

I told him, "Go up onto the battlements and look down into the temple grounds and let me know whatever you see there."

I should repeat here that the temple is a noisy place during the Passover season. The courts built by King Herod are crowded with lowing cattle and bleating sheep, all terrified by the smell of blood that permeates the air. Among those poor beasts are the men who sell them to the Jews who want to offer sacrifices to their god. Grouped together elsewhere are the tables of money changers who are busily exchanging Jewish money for foreign coinage brought by pilgrims from Egypt and Syria and Babylonia and other lands. This service is provided because foreign money cannot be offered to their god. Offerings made to him must always be in the form of Jewish money, because it bears no likenesses of any living thing. The coins of almost every other kingdom in the world bear the face of the reigning monarch or some god upon them, and the Jews have that inflexible commandment against graven images which makes all foreign money unacceptable to their priests.

After a while, my chief assistant came back to me and told me, "That carpenter walked into the forecourt of the temple swinging a scourge, and he used it on the men who were selling sacrificial animals. He also tipped over the tables of the money changers, and that sent everyone scrambling around after all the coins. It was very funny."

The next morning my scribe read to me the first of the written reports from the servant of the high priest. In part it said, "The fellow shouted at the merchants and the money changers as he was driving them out of the temple, 'It is written, "My house shall be called a house of prayer," but you have made it a den of thieves!'"

"So now he has infuriated those men who do business in the temple," I commented. "Can they do him any harm?"

"No, they can't," the scribe said. "Most Jews don't approve of them being there in the temple."

"If that is the case, why are they in the temple?"

"They all have licenses to be there," the scribe replied with a sour look. "They purchase them from the high priests."

"So what he just did was another attack on the chief priests."

"And it will really upset them. Selling the licenses to do business in the temple produces a lot of income for them."

Jesus returned from Bethany to the courts of the temple every day to teach there. The crowds of people who listened to him were greatly impressed, and it was impossible for officers of the Great Sanhedrin to arrest him, so the fears of the chief priests and the Pharisees were exacerbated hourly. Time after time they challenged him there. They hoped that by engaging the fellow in theological arguments, they could contrast their scholarly learning with the common knowledge of a tradesman. By this means they expected to reduce the esteem of the multitude for him, but day after day he confounded those pious pedants with shrewd responses.

At last they came up with a question to entrap him that was a forensic masterpiece. They confronted him in his usual place and asked him, "Tell us what you think. Is it or is it not lawful to pay tribute to Caesar?"

If he responded that Jews should not pay the taxes that are due to Rome, he would in effect be advocating revolution. The rebellion of Judas of Galilee had been against the imposition of Roman taxes, and that remained the most likely cause for any new revolt. The members of the mob who had hailed Jesus as their king on the first day of the week were looking for him to lead such an uprising. Some of them were in the crowd around him, and one of them shouted, "No! No! Jews should not pay taxes to Caesar!"

The carpenter knew I would have him arrested and crucified for inciting the Jews to rebellion if he agreed with that man. On the other hand, if he said Jews ought to pay the taxes imposed by Rome, he would lose much of the popular support which had protected him from arrest by officers of the Sanhedrin. Any such recommendation of submission to Roman rule would cause many of his followers to abandon their hope that he was the messiah they were waiting for.

The trap was well laid. He could not escape it. He had to say yes or no to the question they put. He was as clever as ever in the reply he made, but the guile of Ulysses himself would not have availed to get him out of that dilemma unscathed.

Remembering the ruin of Sepphoris, no doubt, and knowing the disasters that would flow out of any new rebellion, he counseled Jews to pay their taxes, but he did it in an ingenious way. He said to the Pharisees who had put the question to him, "Show me a denarius." They did so. He then asked them, "Whose likeness and inscription is this?"

They replied, "Caesar's."

He said to them, "Render unto Caesar the things that are Caesar's, and unto God the things that are God's."

That reply was very wily. He had asked them to show him a denarius, a Roman coin, legal tender for the payment of imperial taxes. It had Tiberius Caesar's graven image upon it, so it could not be offered to the Jewish god. I must admit I was entertained when I heard of how he had dealt with his scholastic adversaries. His disciples were very impressed and represented his answer as profound, and I suppose it was.

Yet he had alienated popular support he could ill afford to lose. It was inferred by most, including me, that he was saying Rome was providing peace and order and prosperity in Palestine, and it was appropriate for Jews to pay the price for those benefits. In short, his answer was taken to be a call to Jews for obedience to authority. He was sounding better and better to me but worse and worse to the Zealots, who were, and still are, determined to bring rebellion and ruin to their land and to their people. With their question to Jesus, the Pharisees accomplished they were after. Their goal was to discredit him with the majority of the revolutionary mob that had greeted him so ecstatically on the first day of the week, and they had done that.

The next day there was another exchange between the Pharisees and the carpenter in the forecourt of the temple. They asked him, "Which is the greatest commandment and which is second?" I think that by then they were simply raising various issues by then to see if he would express some odd opinion that would further impair his standing in the eyes of the orthodox and the Zealots.

In response to this inquiry, he gave the answer they would have given themselves had it been asked of them. He said, "You must love the Lord your God with all your heart and with all your soul and with all your mind. This is the first and greatest commandment. And the second is that you should love your neighbor as much as yourself." That reply was in harmony with the basic doctrine of Judaism as expressed by the great Pharisee Hillel. I took it as additional evidence that he was no threat to the authority of Rome in the province.

Two days before he died upon a cross, he launched into a last denunciation of his enemies. It was a philippic in which Cicero might have taken pride. I shall offer here a few lines from that final speech of his. They are direct quotes from the Christian biography I have of him.

To opponents among his listeners in one of the courts of the temple he cried, "Woe unto you, scribes, Pharisees, hypocrites, for you compass the sea and the land to make one proselyte, and when he is made, you make him twice as much a child of hell as you are yourselves. Woe unto you, scribes, Pharisees, and hypocrites, for you pay the tithe of mint and cumin, and have omitted the weightier matters of the law, judgment, mercy and faith. . . .

"Woe unto you, scribes, Pharisees, and hypocrites, for you are like whited sepulchres, which appear beautiful outwardly, but are full of dead men's bones and putrefaction. Even so you all appear righteous to the eyes of men, but within you are full of hypocrisy and iniquity."

The remainder of his diatribe was all as derisive as the above quotations. And he ended the speech with a direct challenge to his foes to kill him: "Woe unto you, scribes, Pharisees, hypocrites, for you build monuments to the prophets and decorate the graves of righteous men you have destroyed and then say, 'If we had lived in the days of our fathers, we would not have joined them in killing the prophets.' But you are yourselves the sons of those who killed the prophets. Now live up to the example they set you."

He turned away from those enemies and left the temple with his disciples. As they walked along one of the outside walls of that great structure, his friends called his attention to the grandeur of it. He turned to them and said sadly, "I tell you there shall not be left here one stone upon another which shall not be thrown down."

For ten centuries all Jews have existed in the shadow of their temple—no matter where they may have made their homes and their livings. To most of them what he had said was unthinkable, and it cost him more popular support when his disciples repeated it.

In the tumultuous welcome he had been given on the first day of that week, Jesus recognized the suicidal intention of the Jewish Zealots, who were determined to drive their nation over a precipice into oblivion. In predicting the destruction of the temple, he was prophesying that others like Judas of Galilee would raise the flag of rebellion and that Jews would flock to the new incendiaries as they had flocked to Judas. His mind must have been darkened with memories of the days when he had walked as a boy with his parents among the ashes and the desolation that had once been the city of Sepphoris. His phrase "There shall not be left here one stone upon another which shall not be thrown down" was not just a poetic figure of speech. It surely arose out of his own recollections of the ruin he had seen a Roman army visit upon the capital city of Galilee in response to rebellion some twenty years before. His words were simply a description, a literal one, of a total desolation he had himself once seen.

The officer in command of my guard at the eastern gate of the city reported that Jesus looked downcast as he passed through with his disciples to spend one last night in Bethany. Considering that he had just predicted rebellion and ruin for his people, it is not surprising that he looked depressed.

According to the Christian biography I have of him, he said to his friends while on the road to Bethany, "Heaven and earth will pass away, but my words will not pass away." And by that comment he put himself back into proper perspective as a poor deranged fellow with tremendous delusions of grandeur. The idea that any of his words might echo down the corridors of time is of course amusing to everyone who is not a Christian.

On the first day of the week that strange man had outraged the chief priests and elders by making his triumphal entry into the city. On the second he had done it again by driving the merchants out of the courts of the temple. On the third and fourth days he had insulted the scribes and Pharisees and Sadducees in grievous ways. Each day he did something new to appal some element of the religious establishment.

The chief priests met in the palace of Caiaphas to discuss how they might take him by stealth in some private place. His support among a substantial minority of the populace was still strong, so they did not want to arrest him in public as Jewish law required. That might result in disorder and bloodshed, and he might escape in the confusion.

Fortuitously for them, one of the disciples of Jesus proposed to deliver the carpenter into their hands for money.

They responded with a promise to pay that man, whose name was Judas Iscariot, thirty pieces of silver to do that. The following day I was told by my Jewish scribe that thirty pieces of silver was the traditional price for a slave among the Jews. He said, "It was so understood at the time when the prophet Zechariah put into the mouth of our God, 'So they weighed for my price thirty pieces of silver,' and that was in reference to the messiah."

"That is very interesting," I said.

My scribe seemed very excited, and he kept on talking. "Those priests all know Jesus has been doing everything he can to make his life conform to the prophecies about the messiah, and they set that price on his head as an expression of their contempt for his claims for himself."

"That gesture may turn out to be a mistake," I said.

It did, of course. It has become as important as King Herod's massacre of the male infants of Bethlehem in helping to create the legends that are now being heard throughout the empire. If all the fulfillments of prophecies relating to that carpenter's life had depended upon his own actions and those of his parents, there would be very few Christians today.

As I mentioned in my prologue, Herod Antipas lived only a year after Caligula exiled him to Gaul, and he and I, and our wives, had dinner once during that time. I asked him then if he had any idea why Judas had betrayed a man he had followed so faithfully for some three years.

Herod was silent for a moment, as if he had not heard me, and then he replied, "That man was known to be an active Zealot before he became one of the followers of the carpenter. He may well have joined Jesus because he had come to believe he was the messiah and would overthrow the rule of Rome and establish a great Jewish kingdom with himself as the king. Judas may have lost that hope when Jesus counseled the Jews to submit to Rome and pay their taxes to Caesar. If so, he may have decided to get out of a disappointing experience with some money to show for those misspent years."

"That sounds reasonable," I said.

"There are other reasonable explanations," Herod replied. "He may have been convinced by the miracles he had seen the carpenter do that he was in fact the son of our God and could deliver himself from the hands of any captors by calling on his Father to intervene in some miraculous way. Maybe Judas never lost his faith in Jesus. Maybe his purpose was to precipitate events by forcing his master's hand and, by doing that, to bring about the establishment of our God's kingdom on earth."

"Our last housemaid was a Christian," my wife said. "She was a nice girl, but they crucified her in the town square a month ago. Before they arrested her, she told me a lot about what Christians believe. One day I asked her what they think about Judas, and she said they think their devil took possession of him and used him for his own purposes."

"If that is the case," I said, "I don't credit that devil with much foresight."

On the last night of his life, Jesus of Nazareth had supper in a house in Jerusalem with his twelve apostles. This meeting is described in detail in the Christian biography I now have of him. In the course of the evening, he declared to his friends, "One of you will betray me."

They all were aghast. Every one of them was concerned that it might be himself who would do it. One by one they asked him, "Is it I?" Each of them except Judas imagined the betrayal would be inadvertent and wanted to be given reassurance that it would not be he who bore that awful responsibility. Before they had finished eating, Jesus indicated to one or two that it would be Judas, but he did not tell them it would be a willful act. If he had done so, they undoubtedly would have done everything they could to keep Jesus away from his usual retreats, where Judas could find him.

The account says the carpenter privately said to Judas, "What you are going to do, do quickly."

This last supper of Jesus and his twelve apostles was quite a transcendental affair. He declared that the bread was his flesh and the wine was his blood. He told them they must reenact the event in his memory after his death. It is the repetition of this mystical rite that has given rise to the belief that the Christians drink blood in their worship services, and that is a belief which they themselves share. They drink their wine on such occasions in the belief that it has been transmuted into the carpenter's blood.

The account of what he said to his disciples after that dinner is truly poetic. It describes a last farewell to friends who had loved him as few men are ever loved, but are betrayed as many men are betrayed. In part he said, "Let not your hearts be troubled. You believe in God, believe also in me. In my Father's house are many mansions. I go to prepare a place for you, and if I go to prepare a place for you, I will come again and receive you unto myself, that where I am you may be also.

"In a little while the world will see me no more. Peace I leave with you, my peace I give unto you. So the world may know I love the Father, and as the Father has given me direction, even so will I do as he commands.

"A new commandment I give unto you, that you love one another, even as I have loved you.

"Arise. Let us go hence."

If he had wanted to, he could still have lived. He could have hidden in any one of a thousand places in the city until morning. He was probably still safe from arrest in the streets during the daylight hours by the officers of the chief priests, and he had not yet done anything that would cause me to send soldiers to take him into custody. When morning came, he could then have escaped with a company of friends down the road to Jericho. Being an active man in good health, he could have been across the Jordan River before nightfall, and there he would have been in Perea, within the realm of Herod Antipas, where he had always been safe in the past.

But that was not his purpose. Having decided that it was his tremendous destiny to die for all mankind, he went out the eastern gate of the city and across the brook Kidron to an olive orchard on the nearest slope of the Mount of Olives. That grove is known as the Garden of Gethsemane. *Gethsemane* is an Aramaic word. It means "oil press." The place is so called for the obvious reason: there is an olive oil press there.

That quiet orchard was where Judas expected Jesus to go that night, and Jesus knew it. So he walked in among the olive trees there with three of his close friends, and he knelt down and prayed to his god.

After a while all three of his friends fell asleep. He kept praying until Judas came into the grove leading a mob of men armed with swords and staves. Among that crowd were temple guards who had been ordered by the chief priests to seize Jesus.

Judas said, "Master, master," to him and identified him to the temple guards with a kiss, and Jesus replied sadly, "You betray me with a kiss?"

There was a brief skirmish then, and one of the companions of Jesus, the Galilean fisherman named Peter, slashed at a servant of the high priest with a sword, cutting off one of the man's ears.

Jesus said to Peter, "Put away your sword. Those who live by the sword shall die by the sword. If I wished, I could pray to my Father and he would send legions of angels to set me free, but how then could the Scriptures be fulfilled?"

According to the biography of the carpenter I have referred to, his three friends fled into the night, and he put the ear of the high priest's servant back onto his head, and you surely have to be a Christian to believe that.

The crowd of armed men then bound Jesus and took him away toward the battlements of the dark city.

SIX

The Affairs of Men

*L*ucius Aelius Sejanus was executed two years before Jesus of Nazareth came into Jerusalem for the last time. I had been anxious about what might become of me ever since I had received word from Rome that Tiberius Caesar had gone before the senate and denounced his chief prefect as a traitor and demanded his death.

Sejanus had been my friend of course, or I never would have received my appointment as governor of Judea, Samaria, and Idumea. My wife and I knew his wife and children well, and it grieved us to think of their being thrown off the Tarpeian Rock.

The Roman law which requires the execution of all the immediate family of a traitor is justifiable as a deterrent to treason. However, the law that forbids the execution of a virgin is quite indefensible. The two lovely young daughters of Sejanus, whom my wife and I had seen grow up, were guilty of no crime at all. To us the thought that they were both raped by all their guards, as is the rule in such cases, before they were taken out to be thrown off the rock was very distasteful. If that pair of innocent girls had to die with their father for the sake of the state, they should have been allowed to die with some dignity.

Prior to the execution of Sejanus and his family and many of his friends, the government of Rome was in good order. New strains in the structure of the empire were being dealt with as they became apparent. By then the emperor had given himself up to his infamous nightly debaucheries with young men and women and little children in his palace on Capri.

The imperial government soon fell into disarray as a result of the decision of the emperor to believe the accusations against the man he had entrusted to rule the world for so many years. The enemies of Sejanus had hoped to bring him down and set up one of themselves in his place, but that could not be. Grown senile and suspicious, the emperor never again trusted anyone else with such broad powers.

Before his downfall Sejanus had been detested by the senators and by most other patricians for the power he had exercised over them. They also hated his friends and his appointees. So my own situation as procurator of Judea, Samaria, and Idumea had become tenuous, to say the least. The enemies of Sejanus would ruin me as soon as I gave them any excuse they could use to do it.

In Galilee and Perea, Herod Antipas still ruled as tetrarch, as he had done for thirty years and more. He had tried to enhance his reputation by restoring Sepphoris on a grander scale, as I have mentioned in an earlier chapter, but the project only reminded his subjects of the destruction worked upon the old city by the Roman army after he asked them to put down the rebellion led by Judas of Galilee. In time he overshadowed this project with a greater one, the erection of his new capital city on the western shore of the Sea of Galilee. He called it Tiberias, as a tribute to Tiberius Caesar, and he caused the sea to be renamed the Lake of Tiberias, also in honor of the emperor. As I mentioned earlier, the new city was built in part upon an old cemetery, and religious Jews would not go there, and they deplored the idea of a Jewish capital city that no good Jew could enter.

By the time Jesus of Nazareth led his band of disciples out of Capernaum and began to wander around the countryside of Galilee with them, the throne of

ries he had been hearing about the carpenter from Nazareth. He publicly expressed a desire to see him, but Jesus would not come to his palace, so Herod did not meet him until the day he was crucified.

Perhaps I should explain here what finally put an end to the long reign of Herod Antipas. Three years after I was sent back to Rome by Vitellius, the tetrarch made a serious mistake. At the urging of his wife, he went to Rome to ask Caligula to raise him to the rank of monarch, an honor that had been accorded to his nephew Herod Agrippa I when the younger man succeeded his father as ruler of Iturea and Trachonitis. Agrippa had been able to coax the more royal title out of the emperor because they were friends. In fact, Agrippa had been raised in Rome as a childhood companion to Claudius Caesar, and he had remained there after he reached manhood, and during those years he was kind to Caligula when a lot of other people, including his uncle Tiberius, were not being at all kind to him. Agrippa used this friendship to his advantage very well. He sent word to Caligula that his uncle was conspiring with foreign enemies against Rome. So instead of receiving any further honors from Caligula, Herod was banished to Lugdunum, and all his dominions were awarded to Agrippa, who finally became the ruler of all Palestine and was the last king of the Jews, though his reign lasted for only a few years.

By the time Jesus came to trial before me, all appointees of Sejanus were wondering when they would be called back to Rome and tried before Tiberius on some spurious charge and thrown off the Tarpeian Rock with their families.

The problems any Roman governor of Judea, Samaria, and Idumea would have had to face during that time were serious ones. Direct Roman rule had been established twenty years earlier, when Augustus Caesar deposed Archelaus in response to appeals from the leading men of Judea. By the time I arrived in Palestine, the Jews were becoming restive under Roman rule, which they had assumed would be temporary when they requested it, and my appointment as governor upset them terribly because I was a firm friend and loyal supporter of Sejanus, who was the most unpopular man in Judea since Antiochus Epiphanes had tried to make them eat pork two centuries ago.

Seven years earlier Sejanus had enraged all the Jews. He had moved to diminish a lot of the special privileges granted to them by Julius Caesar and Caesar Augustus. In his palace, when he first informed me that he was going to make me their governor, he gave me a lecture on the subject. In part he said, "Those Jews are a problem because they think they are their god's chosen people and are determined to keep themselves separate and apart from everyone else. With the passage of time, other subject nations have been giving up some of their customs and beliefs and accepting some of ours. In return we have been accepting some of theirs. In the process, all the inhabitants of the empire except for the Jews are being assimilated by degrees, and by so doing they are becoming more satisfied subjects of the emperors."

He paused for emphasis before he went on to say, "Antiochus Epiphanes was quite right when he concluded there would be no end of trouble if that fierce religion of the Jews is left undisturbed. What those people could never understand is that Antiochus was just trying to implement policies that would ultimately be in their best interest, and that is what I want you to do."

Considering the public hostility that has killed thousands of Jews in Egypt and elsewhere in recent years, it appears Sejanus was right. Only by a degree of assimilation with peoples around them will the Jews escape eventual destruction—unless their god is in fact as powerful as they say and he sees fit to preserve them.

Sejanus appointed me to govern Judea, Samaria, and Idumea in the twelfth year of the reign of Tiberius Caesar. The day before I left Rome for Ostia to board the bireme that took me to Caesarea, he called me to appear before him in his palace.

When I was ushered into his presence, he rose to meet me. He walked forward and shook my hand. "Don't forget what I have told you," he said. "Those people must be ruled with a strong hand."

"I will remember," I replied.

He kissed me on one cheek and said, "Good-bye and good luck."

Upon my arrival in Judea, I was determined to manifest to the Jews the authority of Rome. An opportunity to do that came when I moved the main force of troops under my command from Caesarea to Jerusalem for the winter.

I issued orders that the legions carry their usual standards bearing the likenesses of Tiberius Caesar. It was after nightfall when the troops entered the city, so there was no immediate outcry. When morning came, the soldiers proceeded to pay homage to their standards as images of the god-emperor, as Roman military units do throughout the empire. Because of the fervid aversion of the Jews to graven images of any sort, Roman legions had previously carried into Jerusalem only standards that bore no such likenesses.

The Jews have always maintained it is an affront to their god, whom they believe to be present there in their temple, to bring an effigy of any sort into the city. As I anticipated, they were in a terrific turmoil that morning.

Whether or not it is an affront to the god of the Jews to take graven images into Jerusalem, it is certainly an affront to Caesar to banish his face from one of the cities in his empire. Therefore it seemed to me a constructive move to terminate this extraordinary concession to the Jews. Only by treating them like other people will we ever persuade them they are like other people.

I was resolved to stand by what I thought was a sound decision when, as I expected, crowds of Jews came flocking down to Caesarea to petition me to remove the standards.

I listened to their loud entreaties for five long days while sitting in a judgment seat in the city square. I explained to them all at great length how any such decision on my part would tend to impair the dignity of Caesar in Judea and elsewhere in the empire. Often as I listened to the clamor of that intransigent multitude, I reflected on the opinion of Cicero that the Jews are a noisy and tumultuous people. As each day passed I expected the crowd to diminish, but it filled the town square every day and became more and more obstreperous.

After night fell on the fifth day of that insolent tumult, I decided I would never see the end of it unless

I terminated it by decisive action. On the morning of the sixth day, I spoke to the centurions in command of my guard. I told them to direct their men to arm themselves and to be ready to follow orders.

That insubordinate host of Jews from Jerusalem gathered in the town square again, and I waited for my guard to take up positions all around the square before I took my place in the judgment seat. When that crowd of Jews started to shout at me about the standards again, I told them, "I am going to order my guard to kill you all unless you stop bothering me and agree to return home."

Those fanatical men shrieked and threw themselves down upon the pavement and laid their necks bare for my soldiers to cut off their heads. They cried out, "We would rather die than see the laws of our God broken!"

Since I am a rational man, I was not prepared for such a wild reaction. Obviously I could not order that such a crowd of men be massacred. Some who were there were leaders of the Sadducees, men upon whom Rome might have to depend as allies in future crises in Judea. The consequences of killing all those men would have been even more grave than the aftereffects of withdrawing the standards from Jerusalem, which would be serious enough, especially in the eyes of Sejanus—and Caesar—if he should ever hear of it. So I had to capitulate to them and issue an order that the

standards be brought back to Caesarea. Those imper-
tinent Jews had managed to leave me no alternative
but to submit to them. I determined myself never to
allow them to humiliate me again in such a way.

Soon another controversy arose that affected my
standing among the Jews. The city of Jerusalem was
outgrowing its available water supply. It had become
clear that the problem demanded a solution, so I
decided to undertake an enormous project: the construction of an aqueduct forty miles long to bring the
water of the Arrab River from near the city of Hebron
to Jerusalem.

It was a necessary work, one of essential benefit to
the city of Jerusalem. It had to be built, and it had to
be paid for. The only funds sufficient for it were in the
treasury of the temple, where they were kept as a
sacred hoard, doing no good to anyone.

When I announced my decision to invest some of
that money for the good of the people of Jerusalem,
thousands of Jews congregated to demand that I give
up the project. I was reproached and reviled whenever
I appeared in a public place. I had by then endured
more than enough personal discomfiture from their
public demonstrations, so I decided to put an end to
such insolence once and for all.

I ordered a few centuries of soldiers to put on cloaks like the ones the Jews wear, and I commanded them to conceal daggers under those cloaks and go out and surround a mob that had assembled in front of the palace of Herod the Great, where I was staying. When I came out of the palace, that rabble began to revile me again.

The time had come for me to make it clear I would not put up with such behavior any longer. I gave the soldiers the signal to fall upon them. A great many were slain and a great many more were wounded. That brought an end to that kind of demonstration.

The water project was carried forward to completion. It now stands as the chief landmark of my administration in Judea. If I am remembered at all by future generations, it will surely be for that great aqueduct.

Pursuant to direction given to me by Sejanus, I took steps to discontinue another special dispensation conferred upon the Jews by Julius Caesar and Caesar Augustus. In deference to their odd prejudice against graven images, the coins in Palestine had born upon their faces and backs only letters—in the form of words and numbers. I decreed that new coins should be issued that would bear the likenesses of various gods. The Jews donate one tenth of their income to their god, and in due time they would have paid all of their old money into the temple treasury, and then there would be no way for them to continue to make offerings to their god, which would be a very good thing. This action of mine also occasioned howls of protest of course, but no one shouted insults at me in the streets of Jerusalem anymore.

By the time I had been in Judea a year, Jews were complaining about me unceasingly, and they have not stopped yet. I have been informed that one of their historians is now charging me with being too obstinate—it seems odd to hear that from a Jew—and the same fellow accuses me of corruption because I used my office to augment my fortune. Why else would a Roman want to be a governor of any province? That self-righteous Jew also accuses me of persecuting his people; and he says I dislike them. That is true enough, but it is not necessary to like people to govern them well. Sometimes it is better not to.

In my defense, I should like to point out that the mutinous disrespect for Roman governors in Judea that commenced in my time has been increasing ever since. Confrontations between the representatives of Caesar and his Jewish subjects have become incessant, and recently Jewish Zealots have taken to concealing daggers under their cloaks and using them to murder friends of Rome by bumping into them and surreptitiously stabbing them. No one is safe from them now, and Rome has fewer and fewer friends among the Jews in Palestine.

A Middle Eastern specter has haunted the minds of Sejanus and the men who have ruled Rome before and after him, and that is the ghost of Marcus Crassus. As we all know, the Parthians inflicted the worst defeat ever suffered by any Roman army upon Crassus at Carrhae and presented his head to their king upon a tray. Also, during the disorders in Judea in the time of Herod the Great, the Parthians descended on that strife-torn land and drove Herod into exile and placed a puppet Hasmonean temporarily on the throne in Jerusalem.

So Rome continued to be fearful of an insurrection among the Jews, and with good cause. Such a rebellion could be seen by the Parthians as one more opportunity to intervene in Palestine, which was of course once part of the empire of their Persian ancestors, and they have not abandoned their desire to re-establish that great empire.

As I have repeatedly indicated, the religion of the Jews was my chief concern during my ten years in Palestine. It was the most likely cause of disorder, because of the belief it advanced about a sacred messiah who would lead a rebellion against Rome. Sejanus was well aware of that problem. In one of his final interviews with me in Rome, he said, "You must find ways to dampen the pride of those people."

When I ordered troops from the Fortress Antonia to exterminate a chaotic crowd of Galilean pilgrims in the temple, no difficulties ensued, because Sejanus was still in charge of the empire, and what I had done was in line with his directions to me.

Yet it was the same sort of action on my part that resulted in my removal from office and exile. It all took place long after my friend and protector had been thrown off the Tarpeian Rock with his wife and children. For some time his enemies had been getting rid of his appointees one at a time, and they were looking for any excuse to dispose of me.

How it finally occurred was the result of a tumult raised in Samaria by a self-styled prophet. This pretender promised to show his listeners some sacred objects he said he had found on the top of Mount Gerizim. He said they had been deposited there by Moses. In response to that charlatan's call, a throng of Samaritans assembled at a village called Tirabatha to follow him up their holy mountain. It seemed likely that the fellow had planted counterfeit relics of some sort on the mountain. Why else would he be determined to get that crowd up onto it? And what did he have in mind when he finally showed them whatever he had hidden there? Did he intend to lead another rebellion?

The movement of those religious fanatics clearly portended a danger to the state, so I sent cavalry to close off all roads into and out of Tirabatha. When that was done, I sent orders to those troops to attack the mob. Most of the men at Tirabatha were killed, and most of the women were taken captive and sold as slaves. The leader was of course executed, and I felt I had dealt with that situation very well.

However, as I have pointed out, the enemies of Sejanus were still rooting his appointees out of office, and they were looking for any kind of justification to deal with me. Lucius Vitellius had become president of Syria by having his son succumb to the emperor's lust for handsome young men, but he needed to cultivate the leaders of the new ruling party. So when the Samaritan senate sent an embassy to him accusing me of murder, he sent me to Rome to respond to their charges before Tiberius.

Even though the emperor had become so senile and decrepit by then, I was sure he would remember I was a friend of Sejanus, and as we boarded the ship that was to take us to Ostia, I told my wife I was sorry I was taking her to her death. However, the outcome was not so bad for us as my enemies expected it would be. When we landed at Ostia, we heard Tiberius had been smothered in his bed. Caligula had become emperor, so it was before him that my wife and I were

SEVEN

I Am He

*A*t the time Jesus of Nazareth was being led into the city by the men who had captured him, my wife and I were having our supper in the ornate room where Herod the Great had usually dined. As we were finishing our final course, an officer of my household guard entered the room and said to me, "There is an old Jew at the front gate. He says his name is Uriah, and he wants to see you."

"Bring him in," I said.

The officer turned and left the room.

"I don't like that greedy old man," my wife said.

"I don't like him either," I replied, "but I'm sure he hasn't come just to make a social call."

This Uriah was a cynical old miser whom I had made very rich by appointing him to be a publican and by giving him the entire city of Lydda as his jurisdiction to tax. He had made it worth my while to do that of course, so we had an interest in each other's well-being.

The officer had a scornful look on his face when he returned with Uriah.

As he came into that great room, Uriah said to us, "Peace be unto you."

"You may go," I said to the soldier, and I remained lying on my couch, as my wife did on hers.

Uriah looked at me and said, "I came here to pass along some information to you, and I don't think anyone else should hear it."

"I keep nothing from my wife," I replied. "Whatever you might tell me, I will discuss with her after you leave."

She asked him, "Would you like a cup of wine? It is a good red vintage from Galilee."

He nodded.

She sat up and said, "You may sit next to me." It was good of her to say that and to offer him wine, considering how she felt about him. She reached for the bottle on the table and began to pour wine into the cup she had herself used.

He sat on the other end of her couch from her, and I sat up to listen to him.

My wife passed to him the cup of wine she had just filled, and he accepted it and said, "It is a good thing that Archelaus was deposed by Caesar Augustus and Judea became a Roman province."

"It was certainly a good thing for you," I replied.

"I prefer Roman statesmen to Jewish tyrants," he said, and he took a sip of his wine.

"All the publicans I've appointed feel the same way," I said. "At least that's what they tell me."

He took another sip of his wine and added, "And I'm certainly glad Caesar deprived the Great Sanhedrin of the authority to hear civil suits and criminal cases."

"I'm sure you are," I said.

He ignored that jibe, as he had ignored the others. He went on, "A court made up of priests and elders and rabbis should only be allowed to act as a religious tribunal. It was right to put an end to their jurisdiction over temporal matters. And it was also right to deprive those self-righteous hypocrites of the power to inflict the death penalty."

"They weren't actually deprived of that power," I said to him. "They can find a man guilty of heresy and stone him."

"Not without your approval," Uriah replied.

"But that approval has never been denied," I said.

"Do they really stone men for heresy?" my wife asked.

"That is the penalty their law prescribes," I replied.

"This carpenter who has been saying he is the son of our God," Uriah said. "The Sadducees want to get rid of him."

"I'm sure they do," I replied. "They will surely arrest him and try him, if he doesn't leave Jerusalem."

"They will arrest him, but they won't want to try him," Uriah said. "There are thousands of Jews here in the city to celebrate Passover, and it's possible that carpenter has more support than the priests have among them, and if that turns out to be true, the effect upon the priests could be devastating. They are going to want to dispose of the carpenter quickly."

"So?" I said.

"So it takes time to do what has to be done before a man can be put on trial as an apostate before the Council of Seventy."

"I suppose it takes a day or two to get all seventy members of the Great Sanhedrin together," my wife said.

"Even so," Uriah responded. "I'm told they expect to take him prisoner tonight, and they'll want to be rid of that fellow as soon as possible."

"This is all very interesting," I said to him, "but how does it affect me?"

"They will want to have him tried and condemned and executed tomorrow, and they can't try a man on the day before the sabbath even if they could get the court together, because our law provides that a guilty verdict cannot be rendered on the same day as the trial."

"Is that so?" my wife asked.

"Our law states, 'A judge must delay his decision and let it rest all night, that he may winnow out the truth.' And rendering a judgment is a work prohibited on the Sabbath."

"Like throwing stones to kill a man is," I said.

"That's right," Uriah said to my wife as if he were expecting her approval for the rectitude of his people. "Executions are also prohibited on the Sabbath."

"Would you like some more wine?" my wife asked him.

He shook his head, rather impatiently, I thought, and he said, "There are a lot of other complications relative to a formal trial for heresy. An apostate must be condemned by a lower court before he can be prosecuted before the Great Sanhedrin. The priests want to avoid all that sort of thing. They believe the carpenter is a false prophet and intends to lead a rebellion."

"How do I fit into all this?" I asked him.

"It would be many days before he could be condemned to death as a heretic, perhaps perilous days for them."

"What is it that you came to tell me?" I asked.

"I came to tell you they are going to bring him to you tomorrow and ask you to crucify him." Having said that, Uriah finished his wine and left us.

In the days before I left Jerusalem to return to Caesarea, I was told by informers what happened to the carpenter after he was arrested that night. The account in the biography of him that has come into my hands agrees with my memory of those reports, and the following is based upon both.

As soon as Caiaphas was informed that the carpenter had been apprehended, he sent messengers out to some trusted members of the council, calling on them to come at once to his palace. Those men, who were all priests and elders, were summoned to meet and conduct a highly irregular inquest. Their purpose was to interrogate the prisoner and to use the answers he gave to establish him as a false prophet, although it was not their intention to bring that charge against him when they brought him before me in the morning. That night they just wanted to collect proof that the man was a heretic, proof they could present to the Jewish people. By the way, I never heard that the Pharisees, with whom he had often exchanged public insults, were involved in these proceedings against the carpenter. In the category Pharisees, I include the rabbis of the synagogues, of course.

After the temple guards had laid their hands on the carpenter, they bound his hands together with a few feet of rope. Then they marched him into the city and through the streets to the house of the former high priest Annas. The temple guards dragged him into the house and into a room where Annas was sitting in a big chair.

Annas remained in his chair as he questioned Jesus at length about his teachings, but he got no answers to any of his questions.

When at last the old high priest fell silent, the carpenter said, "I have spoken openly for everyone to hear. I have taught in the synagogues and in the temple. I have never said anything to anyone in secret, so why do you ask me? Question those who have heard me." He was aware of course that Annas and Caiaphas had sent many men to hear him and report back to them everything they had heard him say.

One of the guards standing by him struck him in the face and said, "You will not answer the high priest that way."

Jesus said to the man, "If I have said anything wrong, you can bear witness to it. If I haven't, why do you strike me?"

Annas told the guards to take their prisoner to the palace of Caiaphas, where the priests and elders were assembling. I later was told by one of my informers that only a score of the council were called upon to show up there.

The high priest himself presided over that unofficial inquest. Sadducees had often gone to hear Jesus, at times when he had spoken in the courts of the temple, and some of those men were called in to testify against him, to affirm he had been guilty of blasphemy there. Jewish law requires that two witnesses be found who agree in their accusations in such cases. The accounts of the witnesses who appeared against him did not agree entirely. I suppose they were all trying to improve on the truth, to make their testimony more damaging to the accused.

At last two men came forward who swore the carpenter had said, "I will destroy this temple made with hands, and within three days I will build another not made with hands."

Christians say he was speaking figuratively, referring only to his own body when he used the term *temple.* They also maintain that the witnesses misrepresented what he actually had said and that he had never asserted he would destroy it himself.

If the reports of the witnesses were true and the statements made by Jesus were to be taken literally, he had certainly made an absolute claim of divinity for himself. However, the testimony of these two men was not consistent in all details and would not have been admissable evidence in a trial before the Great Sanhedrin.

During all of these accusations, the carpenter stood quietly before them, making no replies. The charges being leveled against him all had to do with apostasy. He knew that informal gathering of priests and elders did not have authority to pronounce judgment on such charges, and he did not choose to respond to accusations falsely made by enemies.

If this proceeding had been a duly authorized trial for heresy before the Great Sanhedrin in the Court of Hewn Stones (which was the only place that court could be lawfully convened), the accused carpenter should have been declared not guilty. His arms should have been untied then and there, and he should have been turned out into the streets a free man. However, it was not such a trial.

Having failed to produce any admissable evidence that Jesus was a heretic, Joseph ben Caiaphas stood up and walked forward to him. In his priestly regalia he stood face to face with Jesus, and he said, "I adjure you by the living God that you tell us if you are the christ, the son of God."

The carpenter stared back into the eyes of Caiaphas silently for a moment. Then he did what he had evidently come to Jerusalem to do. He committed suicide.

He did it by saying, "I am he."

This is an answer that cannot really be appreciated by anyone who is not a Jew. The phrase "I am he" has tremendous connotations, as I have mentioned earlier in this account. It appears repeatedly in Jewish scriptures, but only as it comes from the mouth of their god himself. A typical passage is "I am he and there is no other god beside me." And another example is "I am he who blots out your transgressions for my own sake."

The carpenter's words horrified his hearers, as he knew they would. He horrified them even further by saying to Caiaphas, "And you shall see the Son of God sitting on the right hand of power and coming in the clouds of heaven." These dramatic figures of speech were quotations from a description by their ancient writer Daniel of the coming of their messiah.

Caiaphas turned to the priests and elders who were present in the room, and he rent his robes, as he would have done at a trial for apostasy when pronouncing a guilty verdict. "What need have we for witnesses?" he cried out. "You have heard his blasphemy. What is your opinion?"

Every one of the men who were present agreed he was worthy of death as a heretic. By the way, when a unanimous verdict of guilty is rendered by the seventy members of the Great Sanhedrin in a real judicial proceeding, it results in the release of the accused. The Jews have a peculiar law that says any unanimous decision by that large council is evidence the court has been tampered with. Therefore they always have to make sure one of the seventy members votes to acquit any heretical Jew they want to stone to death.

Some months earlier Jesus had said to his disciples in Galilee that his life would not be taken from him, that he would lay it down, and that is what he did when he made that defiant reply to the high priest.

There is a passage of Jewish scripture that must have been in the mind of the carpenter that night. It is in a book called The Wisdom of Solomon, and it ascribes these thoughts to wicked men:

"'Let us therefore lie in wait for the just man, because he is not for our turn and is contrary to our doings, and he upbraideth us with transgressions of the law, and he divulgeth against us the sins of our way of life. He boasteth that he hath knowledge of God and calleth himself the son of God. . . . We are esteemed by him as triflers and he abstaineth from our ways as from filthiness, and he preferreth the latter end of the just and glorieth that he hath God for a father. Let us see then if his words be true, and let us prove what shall happen to him, and we shall know what his end shall be. For if he be the true son of God, God will defend him from the hands of his enemies. . . . Let us condemn him to a most shameful death, for there shall be no respect had unto him by his words.' These things they thought and were deceived, for they did not know God's hidden plan."

I am sure this passage was in the mind of the carpenter that night because he seemed to be aware of every scriptural reference that might be applied to himself, and he often declared they were all being fulfilled by events in his life. Those learned Sadducees who illegally sat in judgment of him that night must also have been thinking of those words from The Wisdom of Solomon and of how Jesus must be despising them all if he believed the tremendous blasphemies he had just uttered. So they showed him how much they despised him by spitting in his face and punching him with their fists. Then they blindfolded him, and they struck him in the face one after another, and each one said, "Prophesy, O Christ, who just struck you?" That seemed a great joke to the servants of the high priest who were in the room, so they also struck him and said the same thing.

Jesus was held all that night in the basement of the palace of Caiaphas until he could be brought before me in the morning.

When dawn came, Judas Iscariot appeared at the door of that house and hammered on it with both fists.

When a priest opened the door, Judas took out of his robe the thirty pieces of silver he had received for betraying the carpenter and tried to give it to the priest, moaning, "I have betrayed an innocent man."

"That is your problem," the priest said to him. "You look to it."

The priest closed the door and Judas cried out in dismay. He went from there up to the temple, where he threw the thirty pieces of silver through the gate onto the stone floor. Then he ran away and hanged himself from a tree just outside the city.

By so doing, he became the first of many to die on account of Jesus of Nazareth.

EIGHT

The Trial

The day the carpenter died is as clear in my memory now as it ever was. On that morning the sun was bright and warm as I walked up the old narrow street from the palace of Herod the Great to the Fortress Antonia with my escort of soldiers. After I went through the main outer gate of that great stone stronghold, I passed into the hall of judgment and walked up the long flight of stairs to the chamber where I performed my duties as governor whenever I was in Jerusalem.

As I opened the door into that room, I saw my chief assistant standing in the middle of the floor. He had with him a dirty old beggar who was one of our paid informers. My man said to me, "This fellow has some information you ought to hear."

I walked past them and sat down in my chair.

The beggar spoke up loudly. "Last night I saw a party of men going through the streets. They were carrying swords and staves, so I asked them where they were going, and they said they were on the way to arrest the carpenter. I joined them, and we found him among the olive trees in the Garden of Gethsemane. He was there with some friends who tried to fight us off, but he told them to stop. We took him to the house of the old high priest, and most of us stayed outside when they took him in there. After he'd been inside for a while, he was brought out, and then we took him to the house of Joseph ben Caiaphas. Most of us were left outside again, and I watched that house, and I saw a score of priests and elders arrive after we did. They went inside, and they stayed there for an hour. As they were leaving, I asked an elder what had happened inside, and he told me the men present, who were, he said, all members of the Great Sanhedrin, had decided the man was a heretic and should die for it, so they are planning to bring him here sometime this morning, because they want you to kill him for them."

With a wave of one hand I dismissed the fellow, and as he left the room, I heard men talking to each other outside, so I went with my chief assistant to one of my narrow windows, and we saw a crowd of Jews in the street below. It included some who were wearing the robes of priests. There were also a few well-dressed and well-fed laymen, whom I took to be elders, and there were a lot of ordinary fellows in dark woolen robes of the kind usually worn by servants among the Jews. In the forefront of that mob were about a dozen guards from the temple, and two of them were holding the carpenter by his arms, which were still bound together at the wrists. They had stopped him outside the street door of the hall of judgment, which was on the ground floor underneath my room. "Here he is," one of the older priests said to the sentries at the door. "Tell the governor we have brought him to be tried."

"If you are his accusers, you should come too." I recognized the voice which made that reply as that of a young centurion whom I knew because his father was a friend of mine in Rome. Evidently he was in charge of the guards of the fortress that morning.

"This is Passover Week," another of the priests said, "and we cannot come into any building that contains unleavened bread."

Yet another priest said, "It would defile us, and we couldn't take part in the feast."

The two temple guards who were holding the carpenter's arms shoved him forward, propelling him into the gate of the fortress.

I went out into the hallway. "Come with me," I said to the guards outside my door, and they fell in behind me in two columns as I started down the long stairs into the judgment hall. There I walked up to the prisoner and took a long look at him. He was standing between two soldiers, who both held spears pointed at his chest. His cheeks and forehead were bruised, and all down the front of his white woolen robe there was a good deal of blood, presumably from his nose, which was swollen, as were his lips. Even so he was a very impressive figure of a man. He was taller than either of his guards, and he looked stronger than they, although he was fairly slender.

When I described him riding his donkey down the street outside at the head of the triumphal procession, I mentioned that his hair was brown and long and parted in the middle, as all Jewish men wear their hair. It had been oiled and combed when I saw him that first time, but now, as he stood looking at me, it was disheveled as a result of the maltreatment he had been subjected to all through the night. His beard also was unkempt, and there were traces of blood in it above and below his mouth. So I assumed one of his captors had wiped his face with a damp rag, though I could not imagine why any of them would want to do that, unless it was to make themselves look more civilized in my eyes. Except where it was darkened with bruises, his face was deeply tanned, as might be expected of a man who had spent most of his life outdoors. His eyes were as blue as the sky, and they were very clear. I thought that remarkable, since it was apparent from the way his hands had swelled below the ropes around his wrists that he had been tied up all through the night, and he had certainly been tormented during those long hours. Yet in spite of that and the bruises on his face and the bloodstains on his robe, his eyes were steady as he stood there looking at me. He seemed to be sustained by an unshaken faith in himself.

The priests and the elders and the temple guards and all the others who were in the street with them had crowded up to the open gate.

I went to them. "What charges do you bring against this man?" I asked them.

A gray-bearded old priest answered my question. "We wouldn't have brought him to you if he weren't a criminal."

I looked that old man in the eye and said, "I've been informed that some of you met last night in the palace of Caiaphas and found him guilty of heresy."

"He is a criminal," that same old priest said.

I replied, "Take him and try him for heresy, since that is the crime you really want to punish him for."

A younger priest said, "It is not lawful for us to put any man to death."

I answered him, "Whenever the Great Sanhedrin has found a man guilty of heresy in the past and has asked for my approval to stone him to death, I have granted the request. Bring me a report that you have properly tried him as a heretic and have found him guilty and want to stone him, and I will approve it for you, as I always have done."

One of the elders said, "We found this fellow perverting the nation and forbidding Jews to give tribute to Caesar. He claims that he himself is the christ, that he is our king."

"You are charging him with sedition?" I said.

"He says he is our king!" a number of them cried.

My chief assistant was standing at my side. He said softly, "They want you to kill him because you can do it more quickly than they can."

"I know that," I replied, "but his only real offense so far was driving merchants and money changers out of the temple courts, and that is a dispute I don't want to get involved in."

"Most Jews agree with him on that issue," my chief assistant said.

"That is why I don't want to get involved in it," I replied. "If this fellow upsets the priests and persuades Jews to accept some changes in their religion, it's not my problem."

My chief assistant said, "Caiaphas thinks the man is going to raise a rebellion."

"I don't believe that," I replied.

"If we try him, it will take us days to dispose of his case!" one of the elders cried out. "We will have to call a lower court into session first and then the Great Sanhedrin, and those proceedings will all be open to the public."

"He still has a lot of followers," a skinny old priest said, "and they will create disturbances."

"You don't want to have the public onus for condemning him to death," I said to them. "What makes you think I do?"

"We know you met last night and judged him guilty of heresy," my chief assistant said to the men at the gate. "So go through your proper procedures and stone him to death."

"He is a traitor," an elder yelled.

"A Roman governor should resist all attempts to make him one of the spiders in any web of religious orthodoxy," I said to those men. "Take him and try him yourselves."

"No, no, no," they cried.

"I think you are making a serious mistake," I told them. "If I try him and condemn him to death for treason, as you want me to do, he will be crucified, as you know, and that is how he has been telling everyone he will die. I understand he's been saying that because crucifixion is the kind of awful death your prophets have foretold for your god's greatest servant."

"He says he is our king," one of the priests yelled. "We are charging him with sedition, and you must try him on that charge."

I left them and walked to my judgment seat, where I sat and looked up at the carpenter, who had not moved since I had seen him last. I said to him, "Are you the king of the Jews?"

He looked at me for a moment silently. Then he replied, "Are you asking me this question yourself, or are you asking it because those men have put it to you?"

I answered him, "Am I a Jew? It is your own people and your own chief priests who have delivered you to me. So what have you done?"

"My kingdom is not of this world." He said that as calmly as if he had been Caesar Augustus speaking of lands beyond the Rhine River. "If my kingdom were of this world, then my servants would have fought to keep me from being delivered to my enemies."

I remembered then that his friends had been willing to put up a fight for him in Gethsemane, but he had ordered them to stop at a time when a skirmish in the darkness there might have given him an opportunity to escape. Therefore the fact that he was standing before me was evidence that his reply reflected his actual beliefs. His prophecy about the destruction of the temple implied a warning against rebellion. So did his counsel to the Jews to render unto Caesar the things that are Caesar's. His refusal to accept a crown on the shore of the Sea of Galilee was also in accord with the answer he had just given me. It was clear that his monarchic claims were mystical and not political. Therefore the man was not guilty of treason.

Yet I recognized there were problems for me if I released him. After all, Caiaphas was my appointee and my close ally. I counted on his support from day to day. He was loyal to me from the time I arrived in Judea until the day I departed.

Caiaphas was certainly on the spot. Therefore I was too. I intended to acquit the carpenter on the charge of sedition, and I wanted to justify that act completely. By so vindicating myself, I hoped to minimize the strain upon my relationship with Caiaphas that must result. So I decided to pursue my line of questioning further.

I asked the prisoner, "You are a king then?"

He answered through his swollen lips very quietly, "It is as you say. To this end was I born, and for this was I brought into the world, that I should bear witness to the truth."

"What is truth?" I said.

Caesar himself might have envied the fellow as he stood there straight and tall, for thinking he knew the truth when the wisest philosophers and men of science have to confess they do not. Such sublime self-assurance is commonly an enviable aspect of insanity. Yet I would not have considered the prisoner any more deranged than most of the men in Jerusalem were it not for the fact that I knew he believed his crucifixion was a necessary sacrifice to absolve all mankind of its sins and that he believed he would rise again from the dead and that he was convinced he was the only begotten son of the Jewish god. I am satisfied in my mind that all those delusions were rooted in the tales his parents told him when he was young. I still believe their insidious influence on him was the only reason he was not as normal as most men.

Cato spoke truly when he said, "In a land where the majority of men are insane, they would lock up those who are not." Jesus of Nazareth was so composed as he stood there before me in his bloodstained robe that I started to wonder if he was the one whose mind was unhealthy—or if I was.

I said to him, "You hear how many things they say against you. Have you no answers?"

The carpenter remained silent, and the expression on his face was inscrutable. His eyes were staring into mine as if he could see through them into me.

I stepped down from the judgment seat and walked to the open gate and stopped six feet from the grumbling men there and said to them, "I find no fault in him."

That mixed company of dignitaries and rabble all cried out in dismay. One of the priests shouted, "He has been stirring up Jews all throughout Judea and Galilee."

That reference to Galilee suggested a way for me to rid myself of the problem those men had presented to me. I said, "Is this man a Galilean?" and that silenced them all. They knew I could hardly be unaware of the location of the town of Nazareth. Finally one of them said, "Yes. He is a Galilean."

"In that case, he belongs to the jurisdiction of the tetrarch," I replied. I was glad of any excuse to deliver that troublesome prisoner to Herod Antipas, who would not be under pressure from the chief priests in the way I was. Herod did not have any of them in Galilee or Perea. They were all in Jerusalem.

Although the tetrarch had come to Jerusalem for the Passover, he would be leaving for Galilee as soon as it was over. Therefore he could afford to be objective in dealing with the carpenter.

I could not actually relinquish legal jurisdiction in the case to Herod, but I could submit the matter to him and perhaps gain the authority of his support for the verdict I intended to render. I assumed the tetrarch would not play the game of the priesthood in this affair. He was never inclined to get himself involved in the enforcement of religious disciplines. Therefore I thought he would see the case as I did and exonerate the carpenter of the crime of sedition. Like me, he would probably respond differently if the charge were heresy, considered by the Great Sanhedrin under due process of law. I am sure he would have kept his distance from any such legal proceedings and let the court take the responsibility for its decision.

I had another reason to dispatch the prisoner to the tetrarch. Herod and I had been at odds with each other for some time. I saw this was an opportunity to make a friendly gesture toward him that he would appreciate. Therefore I told the soldier in charge of my personal guard, "Take him to King Herod."

The guard fell in around the prisoner, six on either side of him, to escort him up the street to the old Hasmonean palace where Herod was in residence. His mob of accusers followed him, and the priests and elders were making speeches at him, saying things like, "Tell us again how we'll see you sitting on the right hand of God in all his glory."

I knew the tetrarch would appreciate my sending the prisoner to him, because he had been anxious to see the carpenter for a long time. Herod did not know he had seen him at times in the past.

As Jesus was brought before his sovereign in the throne room of the old Hasmonean palace, he must have recalled those occasions when, as a boy in Nazareth, he had seen his ruler passing through town in splendid processions. As a prisoner now his feelings were probably no more approving than they had been so many years ago. The old prince, on the other hand, was disposed to be amiable and wanted to be entertained by a miracle.

If the poor fellow standing in his bloodstained robe with his wrists tied together could have worked a miracle for his king, he could have saved himself then and there. Perhaps I should say if he would have rather than if he could have. He was surely capable of doing unusual things. Upon that all witnesses are agreed, but on that day he never wavered in his resolution to do nothing to save himself.

Herod descended from his throne and questioned the carpenter at some length, but he refused to say anything, not even when the crowd of priests and elders who stood around him began baiting him with accusations and insults. They were hoping to goad him into saying something that could be used to discredit him with most if not all Jews, but throughout his time there in Herod's presence he remained silent. His enemies later said that he was moved by their devil to act in that way, in order to appear to be the great man of god foretold in their prophecies. "He was oppressed and he was afflicted, yet he opened not his mouth," their prophet Isaiah wrote. "He is brought as a lamb to the slaughter, and as a sheep before his shearers is dumb, so he openeth not his mouth."

Naturally the Christians do view his silence before Herod as prophecy fulfilled, and I have no doubt that he did too.

The priests and elders who were there accusing him were all scholars and devout students of the Jewish scriptures. They were outraged by what he was doing, by the theatrical role he was playing on that day. They knew what he was up to and were appalled by what they considered the horrifying impiety of it.

As I expected, Herod Antipas felt Jesus had not done anything to deserve crucifixion, so he commanded that the man be arrayed in a purple robe to make light of his regal claims. Then Herod told the soldiers to bring him back to me.

The soldiers escorted the carpenter back down the street to the Fortress Antonia, and the priests and elders who had gone with him followed him. Again they remained in the street outside when he was brought into the hall of judgment by the soldiers.

I assumed my place in the judgment seat, and I saw one of my house servants come elbowing his way through the crowd of men at the door. As he left them behind and came up to me, he said, "Sir, I have a message from your wife," and he handed me a piece of paper that had been folded once in each direction. I opened it. In her beautiful penmanship it said, "Have nothing to do with this just man. I have suffered many things in a dream because of him."

For sending me that missive, she is considered by some of the Christians to be something of a saint. They think she received a message from their god. I am glad if she will be remembered when I am gone, even if it is only by those strange people.

I was concerned by her premonition. Even though we no longer know what gods we should believe in or what religious doctrines we should accept, everyone takes heed of dreams. What Roman does not remember the story of how Calpurnia, the night before Julius Caesar died, dreamed that her husband's image ran blood from a hundred wounds? And we all live with the memory of the penalty Caesar paid for disregarding that warning.

As I stood there looking at that message from my dear Claudia and pondering what it might mean, the men at the gate were yelling, "He is a traitor," at me again and again.

At last I walked forward to them and spoke to them. "You have brought this man to me upon the grounds that he has been perverting your people. I have examined him and I have found no fault in him, and Herod, his sovereign, has found nothing in him worthy of death. Therefore I will chastise him and release him."

I was trying to be reasonable with them, so I added, "You have informed me the prisoner claims to be a king, and you are right in that; he does, and that is a criminal offense, but he says his kingdom is not of this world. Claiming to be a king in some other world is not at all the same as claiming to be a king in this one, and a penalty less than death should be punishment enough for that less serious crime." I paused for a moment and then added, "There is a custom that I release a prisoner to you during Passover Week. Shall I scourge and release the king of the Jews?"

I asked the question in the expectation that there would exist in any crowd in Jerusalem some vestiges of the enthusiasm for him that had been manifested five days before, when he entered the city on his donkey. I was mistaken in that. Word of what was happening in the fortress was just beginning to get around the city. The men at the gate were not at all representative of the general populace, and they cried out like a Greek chorus, "Release Barabbas!"

I did not want to let that man Barabbas go. He had been one of the leaders of an unsuccessful insurrection and had been found guilty of murder. He was a rogue, and the priests and elders there did not consider him a real threat to the peace of Palestine. The rabble with them surely included men who had greeted the carpenter as their messiah on the first day of that week. Having hailed him as a worker of wonders who would overthrow the Roman Empire, their enthusiasm for him had been transformed into disgust when they came to realize he was not going to lead them in a rebellion.

I also saw a few men at the back of that crowd who were stone-faced and saying nothing. I thought they might be men who still believed Jesus of Nazareth was their messiah and the son of their omnipotent god. If so, they had probably seen him being escorted through the streets of the city by armed guards and had joined the crowd, expecting him to deal with the situation in some miraculous way. If he did so, there was no need for them to speak, and if he did not, they knew they would be well advised to hold their tongues in that gathering.

In hopes of hearing someone in the crowd call for the release of Jesus of Nazareth, I said, as if I had not asked them before, "Which of the two shall I release, Jesus Barabbas or the Jesus who is called by some the christ?"

"Barabbas!" they cried. "Release Barabbas!"

I waited for any voice that might be raised in dissent. There was none. They began to cry out, "Barabbas!" again and again.

I held up my hands to quiet them, and I asked them, "And what shall I do with Jesus of Nazareth?"

"Crucify him!" they shouted.

I asked them, "Why? What evil has he done?"

"Crucify him!" they shouted. "Crucify him!"

In the hope of mitigating their hostility toward the fellow, I said to the young centurion, "Scourge him."

"Here?" the centurion asked me.

"Here. I want those men to witness it."

The centurion said to a lean young soldier, "Fetch a scourge and use it on this fellow."

The men at the gate all remained silent as one of the soldiers took from the carpenter's shoulders the purple robe in which Herod had sent him back to me. Another soldier then removed the man's own white wool robe. The lean young soldier re-entered the room swinging a metal-tipped scourge, making it whistle through the air. He laid it across the carpenter's back with evident pleasure while two other soldiers held the man's arms.

As the carpenter's back became red with welts and then with blood, he made no sound. He neither cried out nor moaned, but his body finally became limp.

After the scourging was over, he was being held up by the two soldiers on either side of him. I told them, "You can take the prisoner into the Praetorium now."

The soldiers stationed in Jerusalem at that time were members of a Syrian legion. They were rough men, and they all hated Jews as their traditional enemies from times long past, so it had become customary procedure to let them entertain themselves at the expense of any Jews who had been convicted of serious crimes. The practice satisfied their worst instincts, which might otherwise have found less desirable outlets.

I followed them as they dragged the half-naked prisoner away into the Praetorium. The two soldiers who were holding his arms were keeping him upright, or he would have fallen to the floor. Another soldier confronted him and pressed a circlet that had been plaited out of thorns down onto his drooping head, and blood began to trickle down his face from all the lacerations. Then two other soldiers draped King Herod's purple robe over his shoulders again, and one put a reed into one of his hands as a mock scepter. Then they all fell down on their knees before him and cried, "Hail to the king of the Jews!"

When I thought he looked pitiful enough to arouse the sympathy of his enemies, I said, "Take him into the hall of judgment," and two soldiers dragged him into that place again.

I went before them and crossed the hall toward the open door, and I stopped a few feet short of that crowd in the street. "Bring him here," I said to the soldiers on either side of him. He was still being supported by them, but as he was brought forward, he raised his head just enough to look at his accusers, blinking at them through the blood that was running down his forehead into his eyes. As he was held up in front of them, he was just a tragicomic figure in an old purple robe and a crown of thorns.

I raised one hand toward him and said, "Behold the man."

His misery had no effect upon them. The priests, the elders, and others in that crowd cried, "Crucify him! Crucify him!"

My patience was exhausted. I said, "You crucify him. I find no fault in him."

I heartily wished to put the whole affair behind me, and it would have been better for everyone if I had succeeded. If I had released him then and there, he would have gone from the fortress thoroughly discredited as the self-styled son of their almighty god. He would have been a public joke if he had preached in the streets of Jerusalem after the humiliation he had been subjected to that morning.

He had come up to Jerusalem to die and serve his own strange purposes by so doing, and his enemies cooperated with him to that end. As I look back upon that day, it appears to me that he knew what he was doing and they did not, in spite of all their learning and ecclesiastical authority.

One of them said to me, "By our law he ought to die, because he made himself the son of God."

It was an error for them to openly state their actual reason for seeking his death at my hands, because it did not relate to the charges they were bringing against him nor to any other crime or misdemeanor under Roman law. However, I found myself reflecting upon what they had just said, in a way that would have surprised any person who has ever known me. The bearing of that poor Jew through his agony had been uncanny, almost godlike. I had felt uneasy when I first walked up to him and looked into his eyes, and that very odd sensation had been steadily increasing.

I turned away from the crowd, and I saw Jesus was still looking at me through the blood that was trickling down his face from his crown of thorns. All at once

I was overcome by the eerie feeling that it was I who was on trial before him.

As we stared at each other, I reflected upon my wife's dream. It seemed to me an omen, an important one, and I began to want to be careful about what I was doing. The gods may exist, or they may not, including that terrifying invisible god of the Jews, who is just as likely, I suppose, as any of the others. And all of them seem to have children by some mortal woman. I began to wonder if this impressive fellow could possibly be what he said he was.

I took him by the arm and led him back into the middle of the hall. When we were in front of the judgment seat, I brought him to a stop and turned him to face me. I looked into that silent bloody face and asked for an answer to the basic question in my mind. "Where do you come from?" I said.

He looked back at me calmly, and he gave me no answer. His conduct now also had me thinking of that passage from the Jewish prophet Isaiah: "He was oppressed and he was afflicted, yet he opened not his mouth."

A few days earlier I had had that entire chapter translated for me, along with some other scriptures relating to the messiah. Another part of it said, "He was wounded for our transgressions, he was bruised for our iniquities . . . and with his stripes we are healed." I was disturbed as I remembered those words, because the carpenter did now indeed have stripes. I had just caused them by having him scourged, so it seemed I was responsible for another apparent fulfillment of prophecy about the Jewish messiah.

At last I said to him, "Why don't you answer me? Don't you realize I have the power to crucify you? And I also have the power to release you?"

We were still face to face and only a few feet apart, and he continued to look into my eyes, and it was getting harder for me to look back into his. I was becoming more uncomfortable because I was feeling more and more as if I were the one on trial.

He answered me at last. "You could have no power over me at all, unless it were given to you from above."

I looked toward the men at the gate, and I called out to them, "The scourging this man has suffered is punishment enough for what he has done."

One of the priests shouted, "If you let this man go, you are no friend of Caesar's."

One of the elders cried, "Any man who tries to make himself a king sets himself up against Caesar."

It struck me as ironic that the same men who had just called for the release of Barabbas, a murderous revolutionary, would now threaten me in this way. Yet I was disturbed by it. For it made the issue of what to do with Jesus of Nazareth as serious a problem for me as it was for them.

Clearly, the prisoner was not guilty of inciting rebellion as charged. Claiming a kingdom in some other world is not a capital offense under Roman law. However, the man had indeed said he was a king, and a crowd had tried to crown him on the shore of the Sea of Galilee after he fed them some bread and fish. And he had been accorded a triumphal entry into Jerusalem that would have pleased Tiberius Caesar himself. Even though he had always advised his listeners to observe Roman laws, the Sadducees, Rome's only allies among the Jews, were sure he was a dangerous revolutionary. Ever since Lazarus had come out of his tomb, they had been predicting that some mob was going to crown him in the near future and that he would raise the flag of rebellion as soon as he thought the time was right to do it.

Therefore that cry from the door alarmed me. The priests and the elders in the crowd there were letting me know they intended to accuse me of putting the peace of the province in jeopardy if I let that man go. They were known to be supporters of Roman rule in Palestine, and they could make a convincing argument against me in their representations to Rome, and I had no doubt the enemies of Sejanus would consider their charges enough to remove me from office, and from this world as well, via the Tarpeian Rock.

It would be easy to prosecute and convict me on such charges. Potential disorder in Palestine was a cause for continuing concern to all parties in Rome. No one had forgotten the repeated Parthian interventions in the civil wars there before Mark Antony made Herod the Great the king of the Jews. Every Roman statesman feared the Parthians would again capitalize on any opportunity that might be presented to them to extend their empire. No one wanted another war between Rome and Parthia, except the Parthians perhaps. Rome, as always, desired status quo.

Sejanus was gone, and his enemies were influential in Rome, and I could preserve myself only by suppressing any and all debate as to whether or not I was protecting the interests of Caesar and of Rome. Even though I knew that poor carpenter was no threat to the peace of the province, I had been put on notice that releasing him would be a threat to my own peace, to say the least. So my choice was made for me— against my will—by those obdurate men in the street.

I resented being maneuvered by them into condemning a man I had found to be innocent of the charges they had brought against him, particularly because I had begun to admire him in an odd way. Therefore I took no pains to conceal my feelings from them.

I went to the judgment seat and sat down in it. I then looked beyond the carpenter at the crowd of men at the open door, and I taunted them by calling out to them, "Behold your king."

They shouted, "Away with him! Crucify him!"

I answered them, "What? Shall I crucify your king?"

They cried, "We have no king but Caesar!"

The Jews have a ritual ceremony that they perform when the body of a man who has been murdered is discovered and the killer cannot be identified. The elders in such a community gather and say an ancient prayer: "Be merciful, O Lord, to your people Israel, whom you have redeemed, and do not lay innocent blood upon them."

Then they all wash their hands ceremonially.

Because I wanted to let those men outside the gate know what I thought of them, I called a servant to me and told him, "Bring me a basin of water." As I waited for him to come back to me with it, I remained in the judgment seat. The carpenter was standing in front of me about ten feet away, and as the minutes passed, I looked only at his sandals and feet, which had dried bloodstains on them. When my servant returned with a bowl of water, I said to him, "Hold it in front of me while I wash my hands."

As I dipped my hands into the water, I looked upward into the carpenter's bloody face. His eyes were closed, and his lips were moving as if he were praying. As I dried my hands on the towel my servant then offered me, I

called out to that crowd of men at the door, "I am innocent of the blood of this just man. Look you to it."

My reference to a ritual that is used only in cases
of murder enraged that crowd. One of them shouted,
"May his blood be on us, and on our children!"

That angry cry was recorded by those few of the
carpenter's followers who were silently standing at the
back of the crowd at the gate. It is mentioned in the
biography I now have of the man. If Christianity
should somehow endure, I am afraid that shout may
result in grief for a lot of Jews.

I beckoned to my young centurion friend. When he
approached me, I told him, "Send one of your men to
the officer who is overseeing the crucifixions today
and tell him to report to me here."

After a few minutes an older centurion came into
the judgment hall. He stopped in front of me and
raised his right arm to me in the imperial salute and
said, "Hail, Caesar."

Jesus of Nazareth was sadly looking at me again as
I told the centurion, "Crucify this prisoner with those
thieves I condemned yesterday."

Editor's Note: That Christ was tall and personally attractive is generally
agreed upon. Jewish tradition had it that the messiah would be a tall, strong
man, and Jesus of Nazareth was never faulted by his enemies for not looking as the messiah should, not even when they were disparaging him for
every other reason they could think of. That he was brown-haired and
blue-eyed is a very old Christian tradition, one that dates back to the century after his death.

I remained in my judgment seat,
and the crowd of men stayed at the
gate, but at last they were silent.
After a few minutes a squad of soldiers dragged the two thieves who
were to be executed into that great
hall. Those wretched men were then
taken out the gate with the carpenter.

NINE

The Crucifixion
and What Followed

I remained in my judgment seat, and the crowd of men stayed at the gate, but at last they were silent. After a few minutes a squad of soldiers dragged the two thieves who were to be executed into that great hall. Those wretched men were then taken out the gate with the carpenter.

As through the gate I saw two of my men lifting up a cross and loading it onto the carpenter, I heard someone in the street shout, "All hail the king of the Jews!"

The soldiers jabbed the two thieves with their spears to make them pick up their crosses and move off down the street toward the north gate of the city. All three prisoners were to be crucified just outside the city on a little hill called Calvary. The Greek name for it is *Golgotha,* which, like Calvary, means "the place of the skull." That hill is close to the city wall. It has been used for crucifixions since the time of Varus, when a lot of holes were sunk into its summit so crosses could be dropped into them.

The carpenter went down the street without being prodded, but he had been weakened by his scourging, so he fell down under the weight of his cross. He got up again, and his cross was loaded onto his back again, and he carried it a little farther, and he fell down again, so the centurion ordered an African bystander to bear the cross for him. A considerable crowd was following him. It included priests and elders and scribes, as well as idle fellows of the sort who enjoy observing executions. The procession grew larger as it drew near the city gate, and women began to join it. By then word was circulating in the city that Jesus of Nazareth was on his way to Calvary, and those women were obviously followers of his who had heard that news, and they were crying his name as they fell in around him. They were all trying to get close to him, and they were all weeping.

As two soldiers dragged him along, he said to women who were near him, "Daughters of Zion, do not weep for me. Weep for yourselves and for your children. The days will come when women will wish to be barren."

In order to witness the execution, I was going down the street at the rear of the procession with some officers from the fortress. Even so I was close enough to see and hear all this.

The women continued to wail as we went out through the north gate of the city and onward toward Calvary.

When we got to the top of Calvary, four soldiers stripped one of the thieves and laid him naked upon his cross and held him down. He did a lot of yelling while another soldier drove nails through his hands and feet. They raised his cross and lowered the foot of it into one of the holes. Having finished with him, they did the same thing to the other thief. Both of them were loudly groaning upon their crosses as the soldiers stripped the carpenter, and he also groaned as his hands and feet were nailed to his cross.

The centurion in charge of the executions asked me, "For what crime is this fellow being punished?" He handed me a little paintbrush, and an old soldier held an ink pot in front of me. Another of the soldiers then held up a short board.

I looked down at that naked carpenter writhing on his cross, and I felt sympathy for him. I dipped the brush into the ink and wrote with it on the board, "Jesus of Nazareth, King of the Jews," and I said to the centurion, "Nail that over his head."

The priests and the elders who were present all cried out in dismay. One young priest said, "Do not write, 'King of the Jews.' Write, 'He said I am king of the Jews.'"

I answered him, "What I have written, I have written."

A soldier nailed that board with those words onto the top of the carpenter's cross. Four other soldiers then raised the head of that cross and lowered the foot of it into a hole between the crosses of the groaning thieves.

"Father, forgive them," the poor fellow said. He was then looking down upon the priests and the elders in the crowd, and he added, "They know not what they do."

Those men who had arranged his death were the men for whom he was praying. As they heard his words, they hooted to show their derision.

I was not aware of it, but I had already witnessed some things that would contribute to making the carpenter's departure from this world as portentous as his entry into it had been. Right after the soldiers had nailed him to the cross, they divided his garments among them.

"This robe of his doesn't have any seams in it," one of those men said. He held up the robe for the others to look at it. "It was all woven in one piece. We shouldn't tear it up."

"You're right," another soldier said, "and the blood on it is all fresh. It can be soaked out."

"Let's cast lots for it," a third soldier said.

One of the older priests there shouted at me, "Don't let them do that!"

"Why should I stop them?" I replied.

He cried, "Because King David wrote, 'They parted my raiment among them, and for my vesture did they cast lots.' Ignorant people will take it as a fulfillment of prophecy."

"Yes!" another priest shouted. "You must make them stop."

"I don't choose to," I replied.

In the course of the next few hours, as Jesus of Nazareth was dying what Cicero correctly called the most cruel and hideous kind of death, there were scenes of the sort to be expected. Priests and elders stood at the foot of his cross and jeered at him. Among the things they said was, "Let the king of Israel now descend from the cross." To the crowd they added, "Last night he told us that he is the son of God. If his father will deliver him now, we will believe him."

One of the two thieves taunted him. "If you are the christ, save yourself and us."

The other thief responded, "You should fear God, now that you are yourself so close to dying. You and I are being punished for our crimes, but this man has done nothing wrong." He then said to the carpenter, "Lord, remember me when you come into your kingdom."

Jesus groaned, "Today you shall be with me in paradise."

The Syrian legionaries all laughed at that.

Those battle-scarred foot soldiers amused themselves all that morning by urging the carpenter to come down from the cross and by continuing to shout things at him like, "All hail the king of the Jews!" They were enjoying the day. Ordinarily their diversions consisted of orgies with bad women and sour wine, but they could only indulge themselves in that way once a month, on their paydays, so they were making the most of this break in the monotony of their military lives.

I saw an old woman who was obviously the carpenter's mother kneeling at the foot of his cross. She was weeping bitterly, and I found myself wondering if she was sorry then for telling him all those stories about the star and the angels.

At noon I ordered an officer to stay all afternoon and report to me whatever he observed. Then I left Calvary and went back into the city. I could not spend the whole day watching those men die. There were a number of other things that required my attention that afternoon.

Soon after I returned to my chamber in the fortress, I noticed through my narrow windows that the sky outside was growing darker. I walked over to one of those big slots in the wall and looked out over the city. It appeared that night was falling long before it should. I saw men and women running up and down the street. Many were screaming or weeping or calling out to their god to save them. It seemed to the Jews to be some sort of supernatural phenomenon. The Christians still feel that way about it, for obvious reasons.

I sent for a horn lantern. When a soldier appeared with one, I walked with him all around the fortress to direct the officers to flog any man who did not exercise proper self-control, and to do it at once. It turned out to be necessary to do that to two or three, but that punishment had the desired effect upon the others, who went about their duties silently.

Thallus the Samaritan, who is certainly a reputable historian, says the darkness at the time of the death of Jesus was the solar eclipse of thirty years ago. All historians are mistaken at times, and he is mistaken in this. The lowering of the sky was a general gloom. It deepened steadily for about an hour until the light of day was extinguished. After another hour that blackness began to disperse very gradually. From beginning to end it lasted three hours. It was an odd sort of atmospheric manifestation.

As night was falling on Jerusalem, I was back in my chamber in the fortress, and I was dictating some official correspondence to my Jewish scribe. As I was finishing the last letter, someone knocked on the door. I said, "Come in," and an officer entered the room. It was the man I had ordered to stay at Calvary and observe whatever might happen while Jesus of Nazareth was still alive on his cross.

"Have you anything interesting to report?" I asked him.

"I think so," he replied. "After the darkness was gone and the light of day returned this afternoon, the carpenter cried out, 'My God, my God, why have you forsaken me?'"

"So the approach of death made him finally admit the insanity of his delusions," I said.

"No, he wasn't doing that," my scribe said quietly. "What he was doing was telling everyone he's the Messiah. 'My God, my God, why hast thou forsaken me?' is the beginning of a psalm written by King David. It's one every Jewish boy has to learn in school. And another line in that psalm is 'They parted my garments among them and for my vesture did they cast lots.'"

"I heard that this morning," I said. "When the soldiers did just that with his robe."

My scribe nodded. "And that psalm describes the Man of God in agony: 'The assembly of the wicked have enclosed me, they have pierced my hands and my feet. And all my bones are out of joint.'"

"Are you telling us the truth?" the officer said.

"If he could have, he would have recited that whole psalm," my scribe went on, "but he was too weak, so he could only remind the Jews there of it by calling out the first line."

"So he was still as mad as ever," the officer said.

My scribe responded defiantly, "That psalm also includes this verse: 'All the ends of the world shall remember and turn to the Lord, and all nations shall worship him.'"

"I don't suppose he's dead yet," I said.

"Not quite," the officer told me.

There are a great many earthquakes in Palestine. As mischance would have it, one of them occurred as he was dying, and that also alarmed the superstitious. Even the centurion who was overseeing the crucifixions was unnerved by it and said, "Truly this was the Son of God." When I heard about that, I was disappointed in him. I had thought he was made of sterner stuff.

The darkening of the sky and the coincidental occurrence of the earthquake proved to be as fortuitous for the subsequent growth of Christianity as the star and the other coincidences surrounding the fellow's birth. As I have said before, it was the events that he and his followers could not arrange that have made the stories about him so appealing to common people.

In addition the earthquake was another incident made gravid with meaning by certain scriptures of the Jews. The Christians now quote what seems to be a relevent passage from a Jewish prophet on the subject of the crucifixion of Jesus: "In my distress I called upon the Lord, and cried unto my God. He heard my voice out of his temple, and my cry came to him. Then the earth shook and trembled. The foundations of the hills moved and were shaken."

Later in the afternoon word spread throughout the city that the earthquake had rent the veil that concealed the most holy place in the temple. This report also caused dismay among the Jews, and it was soon given symbolic meaning by the Christians. They say it implies that the death of Jesus opened the way to their god.

The religious hierarchy of the Jews did not want to have those three men hanging on their crosses on the sabbath, which was about to begin, since their days start at sundown rather than at sunrise. Therefore they sent a request that I order the centurion at Calvary to have the men's legs broken to make them die quickly. For those readers who are not acquainted with the procedure, I should explain that it throws all of a crucified man's weight onto his arms, which makes his breathing more and more difficult until he can breathe no more. I issued that order, but by the time it reached Calvary, the carpenter was hanging lifeless on his cross.

The soldier who had nailed the men to their crosses broke the legs of the two thieves with blows of his hammer.

Since all of their weight was then hanging from their arms, they could no longer take in enough air to groan. They could only whimper.

"I'll make sure the king of the Jews is really dead," another soldier said, and he thrust a spear into the carpenter's left side.

The carpenter was indeed dead. His hanging body did not react in any way to that wound, although it did leak a lot of blood and lymph. The commentaries of the three astrologers about the star, the stories of Mary and Joseph about the angels, and those remarks of John the Baptist about his being the lamb of god had brought the poor fellow to an ignominious end.

A respected Pharisee, one Joseph of Arimathea, sent a request to me for the corpse of the carpenter. If he had not done so, it would have been cast into the pit where the cadavers of criminals are thrown with other refuse, and it would have been burned there that night.

I knew this Joseph as a man of wealth and standing among the Jews. He was a member of the Great Sanhedrin, although he had not been one of those men who met in the palace of the high priest the night before. At the time I did not see what harm it could do to gratify him, so I dictated to my scribe a written order that the soldiers take the corpse of the carpenter down and deliver it to Joseph. That decision turned out to be a momentous one, but I want to point out here that the consequences of it were of a sort that no reasonable man could have foreseen.

By the way, writing that order was the last thing that scribe ever did for me, since he did not come back to work the following day. He was later seen among the Christians in Jerusalem.

That evening another prominent Pharisee, one whose name was Nicodemus, provided Joseph with over a hundred pounds of myrrh and aloes, and Joseph had the body of the carpenter wrapped up in linen with those medicines and a lot of spices. He interred the body in a tomb that had recently been hewn into a rock escarpment in a garden that was close to Calvary. To protect that sepulchre from intruders, Joseph caused a great stone to be rolled in front of its entrance.

The following morning, as I was being escorted up the street from the palace of Herod the Great to the Fortress Antonia by the usual detail of Syrian guards, a dozen priests stopped me in the street. One spoke for them all. "Sir, we remember the deceiver said while he was still alive, 'After three days in the tomb I will rise again.' Therefore we are requesting you to command that the sepulchre be made secure until the third day.

Otherwise some of his disciples may come by night and steal him away and say he is risen from the dead. If that should happen, the situation will be worse than before."

I made an additional mistake when I told them, "You have your own guards. They can provide security. You see to it."

They went away grumbling.

That evening Caiaphas sent a messenger to intercept me in the street as I was walking back to Herod's palace to have dinner with my wife. It was the young man who had been making all the reports to me during that week. "The high priest wants me to let you know he's taking your advice," he called out as I walked by him with my usual guard of soldiers. "He has posted temple guards to protect the tomb from meddlers, and today he had some workmen go and seal that big stone into place across the entrance."

When I entered my chamber in the fortress on the morning of the first day of the next week, my chief assistant was waiting for me there, and one of his eyelids was twitching with excitement.

"Sir," he said, "the watchmen who were ordered by the priests to guard the carpenter's tomb all fell asleep last night, and when they woke up this morning, the stone had been rolled away, and the tomb was empty."

"You can't be serious," I said.

He went on, "They say some disciples of Jesus must have come in the night and stolen the body while they were asleep."

"I should have set a squad of soldiers on watch there," I said ruefully. "They would never have gone to sleep while they were on guard."

"Not if they valued their skins," my chief assistant said.

The question of what became of the dead carpenter is a very hot one in Palestine. The positions taken by both sides in that controversy are exactly what might be expected of them.

The Sadducees say his body was spirited away by some of his followers.

The Christians say the carpenter rose again after three days, as he always said he would. Some of his followers now claim they saw him in various places in Judea and Galilee during the next few weeks. Forty days after his resurrection, they say, he was caught up into the night sky from the Mount of Olives. They swear that happened very near the place where he had appeared on the donkey on the first day of Passover Week.

I have heard recently there are some who try to explain away what happened by suggesting that he did not really die upon the cross. They propose that he was either drugged by a confederate into the appearance of death or that he fell into a faint on the cross as a result of the pain he was suffering and came to his senses after he had been laid out in the tomb. They think he was then persuaded by his disciples to leave Palestine on the grounds that they might be able to make a very good thing for themselves out of the apparent miracle if he was never seen again.

That is quite impossible. There can be no doubt that he died. If he was alive when that Syrian soldier thrust his spear into him, he showed no sign of it, and he could not have lived more than a few minutes after receiving such a wound in any case. It certainly did not occur to any of his enemies who were at Calvary on that day that he might have survived. They knew better.

When all is said and done, the only persons who ever claimed they had seen the carpenter after his death were followers of his. Skeptics point out that they can hardly be looked upon as reliable or impartial witnesses.

Whatever the truth might be, I knew the fact that the tomb had been found empty might turn out to have important consequences, so I made a report on the matter directly to Tiberius Caesar.

That was my last official act relating to Jesus of Nazareth.

Editor's Note: Thallus the Samaritan, to whom the author refers in this chapter, was a contemporary of Pilate's and was indeed a respected his-

TEN

Reflections

As I have mentioned earlier in this manuscript, every memory of mine that has to do with Jesus of Nazareth is still clear—in spite of the thirty years that have passed since his death. Each of those vivid recollections seems like a punishment visited on me by some god. Whenever I think of that man, I remember the dictum of Lucretius: "Religion has persuaded men to so many evils."

When Lucretius said that, he had in mind what righteous men have done in the name of their gods to other men, but he may also have been thinking of what some righteous men do to themselves.

The carpenter brought upon himself his own crucifixion. That death was necessary to him to fulfill the predictions of King David and other Jewish prophets about their god's great servant. Stoning him wouldn't do that, so he didn't want to have the Great Sanhedrin condemn him to death in the days to come. Therefore he helped his accusers arrange for me to do it on that day.

As for the priests and elders among the Jews, they were the men upon whom Rome depended for support in Palestine, and they were rich and powerful. He had challenged them in ways they could not ignore without risking changes in the practice of their religion. They thought the doctrinal deviations that he was advocating were heresies that would anger their god and cause him to abandon their nation to its destruction. Most of all, they feared that the carpenter intended to raise a rebellion and thereby become the means of bringing about that destruction.

They were doing what they thought they had to do. Their intentions were as good as those of most political and religious purists. In the time of Julius Caesar, Brutus was known as the most moral man in Rome. Whenever we think of what he did and of what then became of him, we are reminded that unduly virtuous men can be as great a danger to themselves and their own causes as they are to their adversaries.

Yet to be fair, it must be remembered that the chief concern the Sadducees had about Jesus of Nazareth was that he had declared himself to be the son of their god and a god himself. The priesthood of no religion will put up with a person who claims to be a god of that religion. Usually such an individual will be dealt with by ridicule. He will be called a lunatic and laughed at by priests and worshipers alike, but Judaism in this day and age is different. It holds that some fellow who announces that he is the savior of all mankind and the son of their god will be telling the truth. For the last century such maniacs have not been laughed at in Jerusalem as they would be in Rome or Athens. Furthermore, the religious authorities had declared that the miracles of Jesus were genuine, so they could not dismiss him as a madman.

Their intentions were better than their judgment, and in that respect they were like a lot of other overly righteous men. They should not have prosecuted the man for a crime of which he was not guilty. Like so many other self-styled idealists in emergencies, they adopted the position that the end justifies the means. They did not achieve their end. In the long run men seldom do, because there is no final end to anything we do.

In the course of describing the appearance of Jesus before me in the hall of judgment, I mentioned that I came to feel as if it were I who was on trial rather than he. I presume that is how the judges of Socrates felt four centuries ago.

There are noteworthy parallels between the two men and between their two trials.

Like Socrates, Jesus of Nazareth asked basic questions about the customs and beliefs of his people, and like Socrates he defied the priesthood of the established religion in his country. He and Socrates both believed man has an immortal soul. Both of them held there is only one god, who is the wise and just ruler of the world.

The Athenian philosopher and the Galilean carpenter were both effective in debate with the religious authorities in public places in the capital cities of their nations. By being profound as well as clever, they embarrassed their powerful foes time and again.

Both of them were virtuous, and criticism is much easier for dignitaries to abide when it comes from men who are not too pure. Socrates and Jesus both had the option to live, and they both rejected it. Each had the alternative choice of exile available to him. It was offered to Socrates by the rulers of Athens, and he refused it. It was no less available to Jesus. He could have returned to Galilee, or he could have gone to Babylon or Egypt or Italy or any of a hundred other places where Jews live outside of the jurisdiction of the Great Sanhedrin, and his adversaries would have been delighted to see the last of him. Instead he went up to the city of Jerusalem and would not leave until his odd tragedy had been played out to its end.

Socrates maintained that he had a mission, which was the duty to search for the truth and lead men to it. He viewed himself as a spokesman for his god, just as Jesus did. The two of them said a lot of the same things about what their gods expect of mankind. It is often hard to tell the sayings of the young Jew from those of the old Greek.

There is one salient difference between them. The real reason the Athenian authorities decided to silence Socrates was that his political opinions were offensive to them. However, they chose to execute him on religious grounds—as a heretic. The carpenter was executed for alleged political crimes because the Jewish religious authorities thought he was a heretic. It seems to me the fact that the two cases are so precisely opposite in this respect constitutes a further parallel rather than a difference between them.

A common truth applies to both cases. It is that political and religious leaders are willing to tolerate a man of principle only as long as he does not become a nuisance to them.

When notable men are killed by self-righteous conservatives, it is usually for the same reasons. Julius

Caesar was not stabbed to death by members of the senate for his brilliance as a general and statesman, and Caligula was not murdered for his insanity and depravity. Those peculiarities were forgiven them.

Like Socrates and Jesus, both of them died for proposing to alter an existing order of things. Leaders of men often qualify for assassination by posing a threat to the privileged classes in a society.

If a public figure is willing to accept things as they are, he will avoid being loved or hated very much, and he will die in his bed of old age—if he hasn't had the decency to put an earlier end to his life by committing suicide.

Epilogue

*J*ust seven weeks after the crucifixion of Jesus of Nazareth, a disciple of his, the fisherman called Peter, preached to a big crowd of people in Jerusalem, winning three thousand converts to the view that the dead carpenter was the messiah. That alarmed Caiaphas and the Jewish priesthood as much as anything the man had done in his life, and rightly so. That day was a portent of what was to come. Ever since then Christianity has been spreading, and now it is a concern to the men who are charged with preserving the stability of the empire. It has ceased to be a new sect of

Judaism that is just a problem to the religious authorities in Jerusalem. It was transformed into an attack upon belief in all the generally accepted gods when the apostle named Paul got the other apostles of Jesus to agree a person could become a Christian without first becoming a Jew.

Since that decision, the growth of Christianity throughout the empire has of course astonished everyone. The disciples who were chosen by the carpenter are common laborers for the most part, men with no qualifications to be religious leaders. Yet those ignorant fellows have preached their crucified master's message with amazing effectiveness. They have been believed by thousands of people when they have reported seeing Jesus of Nazareth alive again after he was dead and buried. And when they have sworn they observed him rise into the sky, their story has been deliriously accepted by the same crowds of people. They made their listeners want to believe them by saying that anybody who chose to follow Jesus could also rise from the grave and was promised a place in paradise, as was the thief on the cross.

Before long Jesus' disciples were reported to be working miracles in his name, healing the sick and casting out devils. Hardly a day went by without my hearing another rumor from one of my spies about such wonders. I was even brought stories that both

Peter and Paul had resurrected dead men into life. Jews began bringing their sick relatives out into the streets where Peter was expected to pass by, in the hope that his shadow would fall upon them and heal them.

The Jewish religious authorities sent representatives down to Caesarea to express their new concerns. They informed me the pious devotion of the converts to Christianity was frightening. Members of the burgeoning cult were giving away all their possessions and had all material things in common. That was one feature of the new religion that made non-Jews feel very uneasy about it, along with the stories that they drink blood during their worship services.

Those considerations still bother people today of course, as does the fact that the majority of Christians we see now are slaves and poor people—the dirty, the ignorant, the vulgar. The current popularity of the cult among the lower classes is not surprising. Christianity offers them hope of bliss in the next world. They never before have been given any encouragement to expect happiness anywhere.

Because of the imperial decision to exterminate Christianity, it is becoming a secret society. Here in Gaul—as in Rome—the members meet in catacombs to worship, and some even live in those grim manmade caves. The line drawing of a fish that is now seen on walls everywhere is their symbol. This sign was adopted by them because *ichthus*, the Greek word for fish, is made up of the initial letters of the Greek words *Jesus Christ Son of God Savior.*

The Jewish hierarchy have set themselves the task of uprooting the posthumous influence of the crucified carpenter from the sacred soil of their land. They have declared that Jews who profess the new faith are heretics, even though all such Christians at first insisted they were still devout Jews. The first Christian to be executed by them as a heretic was a young man named Stephen. The Great Sanhedrin followed its proper procedures in condemning him and submitted a request to me for approval to stone him to death. I acceded, as I always did when it came to such requests. I was told they did away with him at the foot of Calvary. That sort of irony seems to appeal to them.

Herod Agrippa, who was a very orthodox Jew, tried to assist them in stamping out Christianity when he at last became the king of all the Jews. He was stricken dead in Caesarea after reigning for only three years, and the Christians have been saying ever since that he was the object of divine retribution for trying to thwart their god's will.

One by one the Jewish leaders of the Christians in Palestine have been eliminated. Herod Agrippa, shortly before his own death, executed one called James as part of his campaign to suppress the new heresy.

Another one whose name was James later emerged as the head of the mother church in Jerusalem. After being found guilty of heresy by the Great Sanhedrin, he was stoned to death two years ago. He died with the words of the carpenter on his lips: "Father, forgive them, for they know not what they do."

The priests of Israel began to use another argument to try to discredit the dead carpenter. In Jewish religious law there is a presumption that illegitimate children (their word is *momsers*) are inclined to apostasy. Because it is a disgrace to a Jew to be illegitimate, the fact that a man is a momser is not to be referred to as long as he leads a righteous life. However, when a man has been adjudged to be a heretic, they feel the fact he is a momser should be made public to disparage him.

That has been done. The fact that Mary and Joseph were not married at the time Jesus was conceived has now been made known to every Jew. His detractors claim to have identified his father as a Roman legionary named Panthera. To eradicate his influence among their people, many Jewish priests and rabbis have taken to calling him Jesus ben Panthera. In spite of that kind of ridicule and in spite of the possibility of being nailed to their own crosses, the Christians cling to the belief that their dead leader is the son of the Jewish god.

However, the world in general is skeptical. It does not seem likely to most people that gods still beget children of women in this prosaic day and age, as we are told they did in ancient times when Jupiter sired Hercules and Apollo begat Aesculapius.

From the time I first heard the miraculous stories about Jesus of Nazareth, I decided they could not be true unless he were truly the son of a god. No mortal man could raise the dead and walk upon water. I had to dismiss such stories as incredible, and what they implied as fantastic. A reasonable degree of probability must be the test of the premises upon which government bases its policies and decisions.

However, when he came before me on the last day of his life, I began to wonder if he might be what he said he was. Now, thirty years after and two thousand miles away from the sad scene of his crucifixion, I can be objective about him and the claim he made for himself.

An intelligent man should be willing to consider anything to be possible until it has been proven otherwise. With that rule in mind, I should like to refer to the counsel of the president of the Great Sanhedrin, who spoke words of wisdom on the subject at a time when no one else in Jerusalem was doing anything like that. He was a man named Gamaliel, a leader of the Pharisees, a noted authority on the law, and a grandson of Hillel, the most honored Jewish rabbi of recent times. The occasion for his words was the trial before the Great Sanhedrin of Peter and some others who had been ordered not to teach in the name of Jesus but had continued to do so.

During that trial Gamaliel said to the members of the council, "You leaders of Israel, be careful what you do with these men. In times past there rose up Theudas, who claimed to be somebody, and hundreds of men joined him. He was slain and all who followed him were scattered, and it all came to nothing. After him there rose up Judas of Galilee in the days of the taxing, and he attracted a great multitude of people. He also perished and those who followed him were dispersed. Therefore I say to you, leave these men alone. If their counsel and their work be of men, nothing will come of it, but if it be of God, you cannot overthrow it."

Those words of Gamaliel also provide the best guidance for the rest of us in this matter.

It now seems unlikely that Christianity will survive, given the determination of Nero to obliterate it. If the Emperor does succeed in wiping it out, the counsel of Gamaliel will lead us to conclude that Jesus of Nazareth was a poor mad fellow who misled himself and others into a tragic error.

On the other hand, if it transpires with the passage of time that the church in Rome survives; if the day comes when there are as many men who believe that Jesus of Nazareth is the son of a god as there are who believe that Hercules is; and if it ever comes to pass that there are more people who pray for healing in the name of Christ than there are who pray in the name of Aesculapius; if all those things take place—and not before—it will be time to derive from the wisdom of Gamaliel another conclusion about Jesus and Mary and the angels and all that.